GREENBERG'S GUIDE TO LIONEL H0 TRAINS

By:
Vincent Rosa
and
George J. Horan

Edited by
Dallas J. Mallerich III
with the assistance of
Linda Greenberg

Photographs from the Collections
of **Vincent Rosa** and **George Horan**
Photography by **George Stern**

Cover photograph by
Earl Sakowski of **Mettee Photography**

[c1986]

625.19

Copyright 1986

Greenberg Publishing Company
7543 Main Street
Sykesville, MD 21784
(301) 795-7447

First Edition

Manufactured in the United States of America

Greenberg Publishing Company offers the world's largest selection of Lionel, American Flyer and other toy train publications as well as a selection of books on model and prototype railroading. To receive our current catalogue, send a stamped, self-addressed envelope marked "Catalogue."

Greenberg Publishing Company sponsors the world's largest public model train shows. The shows feature extravagant operating model railroads for N, H0, 0, Standard and 1 gauges as well as a huge marketplace for buying and selling nearly all model railroad equipment. The shows feature, as well, a large selection of dollhouse miniatures.

Shows are currently offered in New York, Philadelphia, Pittsburgh, Baltimore, Washington, D.C., Williamsburg and Boston. To receive our current show listing, please send a stamped, self-addressed envelope marked "Train Show Schedule."

Library of Congress Cataloging-in-Publication Data

Rosa, Vincent.
    Greenberg's guide to Lionel HO trains.

    Includes index.
    1. Railroads--Models. 2. Lionel Corporation.
I. Horan, George J. II. Title. III. Title: Lionel HO trains.
TF197.H67 1986   625.1'9'075   86-3125
ISBN 0-89778-023-X

Table of Contents

Acknowledgments

Many collectors, train dealers, businessmen and other individuals have contributed greatly to the compilation of this book.

Vincent Rosa would like to thank **Bruce** and **Linda Greenberg** for giving him the chance to write this book and to act as production assistant for the project. Special thanks: to George Horan for sharing his extensive knowledge of and writings on H0, which helped greatly to expedite the work; to his wife, **Bonnie**, who helped edit and type much of the manuscript, as well as data sheets and letters sent to collectors; to his good friends, **Paul Summers, Joe Sadorf** and **Carl Sclafani** for their support; to **Dennis Cimino** and **Thom Shepler** whose early listings indicated the breadth of the Lionel H0 production; to **Allessandro Rossi**, president of **Rivarossi**, who kindly answered all correspondence and provided view points and recollections essential to the story of his company's relationship with Lionel; to **Mst. Sgt. James McKinney**, U.S. Army, retired, of Como, Italy, who also lent a great deal of first-hand knowledge of the Rivarossi production. Mst. Sgt. McKinney worked for Rivarossi after the end of World War II. Additional thanks to **Lenny Dean** and **Sam Belser**, two Lionel Corporation executives who shared their recollections for our historical naratives. **I.D. Smith** and **Jack Fulton** offered useful data and suggestions. The following individuals helped by completing data sheets and providing comments and suggestions well-used in the production of this book: **Norman E. Anderson, Larry Backus, Lou Bohn, Frank Brua, Lester Case, Harold Carstens, Ken Fairchild, Fred Heimann, James Kimenhour, T.C. Lasky, Tom McComas, Michael J. Ocilka, Joseph Otterbein, Robert C. Royer, Douglas Ruhl, Jim Stabley, Bernard Stekoll, Joe Tucker, Howard Twilley** and **Gary P. Vitolo**. **Nat Polk** of **Polk's Model Craft Hobbies** kindly provided material from his company's "Blue Book of Hobbies." Additional thanks to **Bowser Manufacturing Co.** and **Railroad Model Craftsman** magazine.

George Horan would like to thank those who have helped in the many hours spent in researching and developing the information presented in this book, and those who helped him acquire the items needed for the photographic illustrations, namely, **Ed Schols**, a long time dealer, **Joe Jerome, Joe Robinson, Ed Timlin, Mike Nechapor** and **Fred Coppola**. George would also like to offer "much love and thanks to my wife, **Betty**, and two children, **Mark** and **Stacy** for putting up with my moods while working on this book. It was a long haul."

Both authors would like to thank the staff at Greenberg Publishing Co. for their efforts in producing this book. Lending her masterful attention to detail, **Cindy Lee Floyd** directed many aspects of this project, including word processing and correspondence with the readers of the manuscript. **Pat Nuse** keyed the manuscript into word processor files. **Dallas J. Mallerich III** edited this book to insure consistency in its form and content and to assist the authors in their presentation of the material. Dallas also provided information from his forthcoming book, **Greenberg's Guide to Athearn Trains**, for the historical narrative in Chapter III. Assistant editor, **Linda Greenberg** made a careful review of the narrative text and offered many excellent suggestions for its improvement. Graphic artist **Donna Price** applied her superb skills to the visual design of each individual page of this book. Donna also read and annotated the text with her useful comments regarding content, consistency and clarity. **David Price** assisted in placing last-minute corrections. Sales manager **Bill Mitchell** provided data from his own collection for use in the listings.

George Stern, Greenberg's talented photographer, produced the majority of the black and white photographs and all of the color plates for this edition. George's tremendous skills as a photographer and darkroom technician are evidenced throughout the book. **Paul Summers** very carefully and meticulously photographed Vincent Rosa's fine collection. However, these photographs were not employed, because a subsequent session, in which models from the collections of both authors were photographed, allowed for a more complete presentation of the material. Both George and Vincent have very extensive collections of Lionel H0; therefore, Vincent brought only those models which George did not have to the session at George's home. Greenberg Publishing Company's excellent staff photographer, **George Stern**, photographed the combined collections, with the assistance of **Bruce Greenberg**, who recorded detailed caption materials on a compact computer while the photographs were composed.

The Authors invite collectors to participate in the collection of additional data regarding Lionel H0 trains. If you have a variation which is not listed in this book, or a question regarding the details of an item described herein, please write to George Horan and Vincent Rosa in care of the Publisher. We welcome all comments and suggestions. Happy hunting!

Vincent Rosa
George Horan
April, 1986

Foreword

VINCENT ROSA

As an author writing on what seems to be an almost untouched subject, I can't help but feel that I am treading on sacred Lionel burial grounds inhabited by the "Great Spirit" himself—Joshua Lionel Cowen, a man whose products have brought pleasure and joy to countless numbers of boys and girls from 1900-1969.

The Lionel name has always been synonymous with Standard Gauge, 0 Gauge and 0-27 Gauge trains—"the big trains" that people remember from bygone Christmas gardens and childhood train sets. Today, many Lionel collectors are unaware of or uninformed about the H0 trains that Lionel produced from 1957-1966. As the latent bug for collecting Lionel H0 bit me, I found myself hunting the train meets for the few pieces I could find. "Do you have any Lionel H0?" and "What do you think of Lionel H0?", I would ask.

Some of the dealers responded very negatively. "How could they be so indifferent or disinterested about the elusive pieces so neatly and compactly presented in the back of the catalogues in the 1950s and early 1960s?", I wondered. In a telephone interview on June 12, 1984, former Lionel Corporation service manager Lenny Dean suggested that "Joshua Lionel Cowen's baby was the 0 Gauge line—Lionel H0 was his stepchild". It seemed that a sizeable portion of Lionel collectors had adopted this feeling.

For many years, interest in Lionel trains has grown rapidly. Today, much of the new interest is focused on the H0 trains. One collector proudly told me that he displays his H0 Gauge locomotives in front of their 0 Gauge equivalents, on the same shelf. "It makes a great display," he said, "They're cute, real cute. They look like scaled-down versions of my 0 Gauge." Regardless of your reasons, Lionel H0 trains provide a fascinating field for the collector. The trains are not only attractive, but they are excellent products, which operate very well when properly maintained. I hope that this book will encourage continued growth in the interest of Lionel H0 trains.

GEORGE J. HORAN

It is my hope that the information provided in this book will help to correct some of the inaccurate ideas that have to do with the Lionel H0 line marketed from 1957 to 1966. My purpose is to provide a guide for the collector and enthusiast. I have spent the last six-and-one-half years listing my own information, as well as the information of other collectors in my area. To aid the new collector in identification of the pieces described in this book, I have attempted to describe the smallest details. I hope that this approach will stimulate an interest in the smaller, less expensive series of Lionel trains and that it will help those who have the interest but not the experience to try collecting.

I have attended swap meets in the states of New York, Delaware, Pennsylvania, Virginia and Connecticut to investigate and gain a first-hand knowledge of the prices these items bring today. I have also used listings from all over the United States and Canada as cross references. Additional information and historical insights have been provided by Vincent Rosa and the many readers of the manuscript. As an added check for the year of manufacture, I have referred to my own cash receipts of the purchases I have made. I have always kept receipts and added the number and road name appearing on the car and its original carton as I unpacked them. I find now that this habit has proven to be an excellent source of reliable information. It includes the Lionel trains and accessories, including the items made by Plasticville.

Lionel H0 is an exciting field of study. Many 0 Gauge collectors are unaware that the loads used on H0 scale loads were often the same ones used on the larger cars. They may even be surprised to find that many of the popular 0 Gauge operating cars, as well as popular road names on the more traditional items, were duplicated in the smaller line. As we shall see, Lionel's trains were manufactured by several producers, who usually did not use the Lionel catalogue numbers on the models they produced for Lionel. Thus, collecting these trains can present some interesting challenges. While the familiar Lionel logo, an **L** within a circle, appears on many of the items, its absence on others provokes some interesting questions. This book will address some of these questions and present others that will create additional enthusiasm for the novice or experienced collector.

PURPOSE

The purpose of this book is to provide a comprehensive listing with current prices for Lionel H0 scale locomotives, rolling stock and trackside accessories, produced from 1957 through 1966. We include those variations which have been authenticated. In a few cases we ask our readers for further information where information is missing or doubtful. Values are reported for each item where there have been reported sales.

DETERMINING VALUES

Toy train values vary for a number of reasons. First, consider the **relative knowledge** of the buyer and seller. A seller may be unaware that he has a rare variation and sell it for the price of a common piece. Another source of price variation is **short-term fluctuation** which depends on what is being offered at a given train meet on a given day. If four 0635LTs are for sale at a small meet, we would expect that supply would outpace demand and lead to a reduction in price. A related source of variation is the **season** of the year. The train market is slower in the summer and sellers may at this time be more inclined to reduce prices if they really want to move an item. Another important source of price variation is the relative strength of the seller's **desire to sell** and the buyer's **eagerness to buy.** Clearly a seller in economic distress will be more eager to strike a bargain. A final source of variation is **the personalities** of the seller and buyer. Some sellers like to quickly turn over items and, therefore, price their items to move; others seek a higher price and will bring an item to meet after meet until they find a willing buyer.

CONDITION

For each item, we provide three categories: **Good, Excellent and Mint.** The Train Collectors Association (TCA) defines conditions as:

GOOD - Scratches, small dents, dirty

Lionel's first HO scale catalogue, released in 1957. Reproduced with permission of Lionel Trains, Mt. Clemens, Michigan, 48045.

EXCELLENT - Minute scratches or nicks, no dents or rust

MINT - Brand new, absolutely unmarred, all original and unused, in original box.

In the toy train field there is a great deal of concern with exterior appearance and less concern with operation. If operation is important to you, then ask the seller whether the train runs. If the seller indicates that he does not know whether the equipment operates, you should test it. Most train meets have test tracks provided for that purpose.

We include MINT in this edition because of the important trade in Lionel H0 items. However there is substantial confusion in the minds of both sellers and buyers as to what constitutes "mint" condition. How do we define mint? Among very experienced train enthusiasts, a mint piece means that it is brand new, in its original box, never run, and extremely bright and clean (and the box is, too). An item may have been removed from the box and replaced in it but it should show no evidence of handling. A piece is not mint if it shows any scratches, fingerprints or evidence of discoloration. It is the nature of a market for the seller to see his item in a very positive light and to seek to obtain a mint price for an excellent piece. In contrast, a buyer will see the same item in a less favorable light and will attempt to buy a mint piece for the price

of one in excellent condition. It is our responsibility to point out this difference in perspective **and** the difference in value implicit in each perspective, and to then let the buyer and seller settle or negotiate their different perspectives.

We receive many inquiries as to whether or not a particular piece is a "good value." This book will help answer that question; but, there is NO substitute for experience in the marketplace. WE STRONGLY RECOMMEND THAT NOVICES DO NOT MAKE MAJOR PURCHASES WITHOUT THE ASSISTANCE OF FRIENDS WHO HAVE EXPERIENCE IN BUYING AND SELLING TRAINS. If you are buying a train and do not know whom to ask about its value, look for the people running the meet or show and discuss with them your need for assistance. Usually they can refer you to an experienced collector who will be willing to examine the piece and offer his opinion.

NO REPORTED SALES

In the few cases where there is insufficient information upon which to determine the value of a given item, we show **NRS** in the price column. Here again we recommend that you rely on your **experience** or on the **assistance** of an experienced collector to determine what price you should pay for any of these items.

Chapter I
Overview: Lionel H0 Trains

Lionel anticipated the need for smaller gauge trains when they presented their 00 (double 0) Gauge line in 1938. "H0, although not quite as popular as 00, was introduced to the model railroad consumer by Bing, a German manufacturer, in 1924."[1] The difference between the scales is slight—H0 is 3.5 mm to the foot and 00 is 4.0 mm to the foot. Regardless of these two small sizes, the king of the model rails in the Lionel catalogues of the late 1930s, 1940s and early 1950s was still their 0 Gauge line. It is interesting to note that 0 Gauge, with its 1-1/4" between the rails was first considered by Lionel in 1915, not only because Ives, its direct competitor had had its own 0 Gauge line since 1910 (according to Ron Hollander), but because they "took up less room and were cheaper to produce" than the wide, hefty Standard Gauge models.[2] Even though the 00 Gauge line sold well, Lionel did not revive this well-running small gauge line after the war. 00 was primarily a modelers' gauge directed at the true model railroader and serious prototype buff. Since Lionel's 0 Gauge sales still represented the company's main income in 1946, Lionel decided to maintain its toy train image where exact scale proportions were not top priority and they could "play" with the lengths and widths of trains. What mattered to Lionel were the looks, sounds and feel of a railroad, not necessarily the lengths, widths and add-on details. Also, Lionel had to consider American Flyer, its direct competitor, which was adding smoke, knuckle couplers and chug-chug sounds to its new, small S Gauge trains (7/8" between the rails). American Flyer, we should note, had produced H0 trains as early as 1938.

In retrospect, we can see that the trend in America followed the pattern set in Europe, where the favorite modeling scale shifted from Standard Gauge to 0 Gauge and then from 0 Gauge to H0. But the executives at Lionel must have felt H0 was certainly not the scale with which to compete against Flyer, because it was too small to mirror the things Flyer was doing in S at the time - smoke, knuckle couplers and action cars were at least a decade into the future of H0 and certainly not the reason why the modeler used H0. The modeler was looking for the detail and exact reproduction of the scene rather than the action and toy-like play value of the train set itself.

Lionel did well with their 0 Gauge line, and in 1953 the corporation sold more than $32 million worth of trains, toys and electrical-related manufacturing.[3] This was the highest sales report in their history - the decision to stay out of the modelers' gauges, like 00 and H0, seemed a correct one. But, in the early 1950s, the marketplace started to change. American train consumers began to buy and demand more H0 than 0 Gauge trains. Tom McComas states in his book **Lionel: A Collector's Guide and History Vol. III** that "Lionel at first did not notice

the inroads H0 was making because in those postwar boom years, there seemed to be enough business for everyone." According to McComas, the combined sales of H0 manufacturers, which included Mantua, Tyco, Athearn, Varney, Penn Line, etc., had exceeded Lionel's 0 Gauge sales by the mid-1950s. The reasons for this change during the late postwar years may reflect considerations of space, cost and sophistication on the part of the postwar baby boom generation. Most likely, the new generation of "baby boomers" and their dads who were weaned on tin trains wanted models that looked like real railroads going through mountains and farmlands all with the same proportions. Lionel's 0 Gauge with its arbitrary measurements looked toyish compared with the newer H0 that was being made.

It is only conjecture to state as both McComas and Hollander did in their books that had Lionel stayed in 00, it might have deflected the advance of H0 into the toy train consumer market. Yes, Lionel's 00 was a small gauge train, but it was incompatible with what most small gauge manufacturers were making at the time. The H0 industry was striving for compatibility so that different manufacturers' trains could be used together, and it was aided by the National Model Railroad Association (N.M.R.A.), which tested the standard "horn hook" coupler design. Thus, 00 trains could not be offered in a field dominated by H0 producers. The small H0 scale models, which were constructed primarily of molded plastic and simply-formed metal parts (or die-cast pieces, in some cases), were much cheaper to manufacture than 00 would have been. By 1957 H0 manufacturers were producing standardized, ready-to-run train sets. This posed a direct threat to Lionel's business because highly-detailed H0 train sets were now directly competing with the less-detailed, mass-produced Lionel train sets that sold for $20.00 or more. You could buy a complete H0 train set with track and power pack for as little as $10. So, price was definitely a consideration when making the move to ready-to-run H0.

Sam Belser, Lionel Corporation's sales manager in the late 1950s, explains that "Lionel wanted to get more of the mass market. People by the mid-1950s were becoming more aware of H0 and the smaller gauges. Many people were living in apartments and smaller homes with limited space; the need for Lionel to supply products to meet this need was there." While the popular notion held that only a smaller scale such as H0 could serve these requirements, Lionel's advertising offered a contradictory message. "In the late 1950s, we were advertising that you could have an 0 Gauge layout on a card table," states Belser.[4]

Ron Hollander supports Mr. Belser's statements in his book, **All Aboard.** Discussing the inconsistencies of the Lionel Corporation's policy towards H0, he states, "The regular Lionel consumer catalog undercut its own H0 sales by warning parents of the complicated wiring and extra gadgets two-rail H0

---

1. **A Collector's Guide and History, Vol III, Standard Guage**,   T. McComas & J. Tuohy, TM Productions, 1978, p. 99.

2. **All Aboard! The Story of Joshua Lionel Cowen & His Lionel Train Company**, Workman Publishing, N.Y., 1981, p. 54. Ron Hollander.

3. McComas & Tuohy, ibid.

4. Sam Belser interview (telephone) by V. Rosa on August 14, 1984.

required. Why buy H0, the catalogue implied, when even a bridge-table top is enough to accommodate a Lionel 027 layout."[5]

In an exclusive October 1957 interview with **Railroad Model Craftsman** magazine, Alan Ginsberg, Vice President in charge of sales, disagreed with the idea that Lionel was prompted to move into H0 by the trend towards smaller homes with limited space. When asked, "Has the trend toward smaller homes affected your entry into H0 any?" he replied, "No, 0 Gauge need not take any more room than H0." Certainly, then, Lionel did not intend for its own brand of H0 models to sell better than the traditional 0 Gauge line. Ginsberg stated that Lionel entered the H0 marketplace for two reasons:

1. Objective evidence of increasing consumer interest.
2. It is an entirely different market than the "boy market."

Mr. Ginsberg explained that H0, as Lionel saw it in 1957, was for the permanent hobbyist. "As for the boy market (mass consumer toy train market), H0 cannot be as dominant as 0 for play value. H0 is for older, more skillful boys and the mature hobbyist." Indeed, Lionel maintained its position, both the Italian-made Rivarossi models sold in 1957 and the American-made Athearn models of 1958 satisfied preferences of the mature hobbyist.

However, 1960 saw a reversal in this policy. In the catalogue for that year, Lionel emphasized "toy quality" with the fanfare, "A first in H0—Brand new action packed operating cars." In this manner, Lionel introduced its operating cars patterned after successful 0 Gauge counterparts, an idea later to be imitated, even exploited by Tyco. That year saw the 0319 Helicopter Car, 0847 Exploding Boxcar, 0850 Missile Launcher Car, 0301 Pennsylvania Coal Dump and 0300 Operating Lumber Car introduced. This ushered in a new marketing emphasis and direction to their H0 line. This definitely was not what Vice President Alan Ginsberg, and Lionel had planned in 1957, when the emphasis was realism, the catch word was detailing, the main concern was dependability and above all, the H0 line had to reflect Lionel craftsmanship. Somewhere between April and October of 1957, a decision that was four years in the making saw Lionel plunge into the H0 train market even though by late 1956, "Lionel's overall train business was starting to sink with sales down to $22 million.... It was time, but, unfortunately, in retrospect, the decision came too late. It is interesting to note that by the toy fair of March 1957, Lionel still had not exhibited any H0. It seemed that another year would pass before a new H0 line could be introduced."[6] The question remained unanswered among both trade and consumer circles, "Why hasn't Lionel introduced a smaller gauge companion to its 0 Gauge line?" The authors believe that some of the old guard executives including Joshua Cowen himself were reluctant. Tooling for a completely new, unproven line meant a sizable investment. Also, Joshua Lionel Cowen was 80 years old and Chairman of the Board, and, according to Lenny Dean, his first love was 0 Gauge. According to Sam Belser, Cowen's son, Lawrence, who was president of Lionel in 1957, "was more enthused about H0 and the company's other diversifications than his father was. The old guard executives felt H0 would just divert energies."[7] According to Lenny Dean, "The top

brass at Lionel felt that they hadn't done all they could do in 0 Gauge yet and 0 Gauge was top priority. But with H0, Lionel felt it could capture at least part of the new market."[8]

Lionel President Lawrence Cowen inspects the new H0 line aimed at the hobby market. **Courtesy Railroad Model Craftsman.**

According to Alan Ginsberg, Lionel's entry into H0 would represent substantial total increases in H0 sales through the attraction of new customers. He believed that H0 was plus business. This he felt would attract more plus business for the industry. He also said that "If Lionel couldn't have come up with enough elements of superiority in H0, we'd have been foolish to enter the field."[9]

It was Alan Ginsberg who made a trip to Italy sometime between March and October of 1957 to contact Rivarossi, an Italian firm known for making high quality, detailed H0 scale models. The agreement was that Rivarossi would make the trains and Lionel would distribute them under Lionel's name and pay a percentage to Rivarossi.[10] This would save Lionel the cost of creating their own dies and tools. According to Ginsberg, Lionel had been studying the H0 field since before 1953 and found that they could enter the field in a dozen different ways. They chose Rivarossi because of its high quality products. He stated that the Lionel Engineering Department had conducted amazing tests with it.[11] But the writer from **Railroad Model Craftsman** suspected that Joshua Lionel Cowen's thoughts during those decision-making days of 1957 must have dwelt on the fact that Lionel H0 was a far cry from the early, massive Standard and 0 Gauge trains produced 50 years earlier.

Lionel heralded its entrance into H0 with a four-page separate folder that they distributed with their 1957 0/027 catalogue. Ron Hollander states in **All Aboard** that Lionel H0 went into production too late to be included in the regular catalogue, but Sam Belser has another interpretation. "I was a supporter of a separate H0 catalogue. I felt we had to create enthusiasm and show that H0 was a vital, viable line on its own. When, in 1958, they included H0 into the regular 0 catalogue, I felt this neutralized the merchandising affect.

5. Hollander, p. 225.
6. McComas & Tuohy, p. 103.
7. Sam Belser, ibid.
8. Lenny Dean interview (telephone), June, 1984.
9. **Railroad Model Craftsman**, October 1957, p. 54.
10. McComas & Tuohy, ibid.
11. **Railroad Model Craftsman**, ibid.

From the very beginning, our problems in merchandising the H0 line came from our limitations in our advertising budget."[12]   1957 was the only year in which Lionel acknowledged that someone else was making their H0 scale models. According to Alan Ginsberg, Lionel's entry into H0 was not just a trial balloon, "Lionel's engineering department was into H0 with both feet and our 1958 development work was in full swing."[13] At the time he may not have realized that the relationship between Rivarossi and Lionel would be short-lived—one year only—and that Athearn of Los Angeles would assume the complete production of the 1958 H0 line.

Rivarossi, then, was instrumental in supplying Lionel Corp. of New York with its first mass-produced, ready-to-run H0 trains in 1957. These highly detailed and well-made model trains are among the most desirable and collectible Lionel H0 trains today and are top quality, scale replicas of real trains in their day.

The Lionel management indicated the quality of the new line produced in cooperation with the world famous manufacturing firm of Rivarossi and bearing the Lionel trademark **L** (within a circle) would insure both firms an extensive share of the H0 scale market. Lionel had won the confidence of the consumer over a period of 57 years and voiced its determination to keep the company's name synonymous with the finest in model railroading.

The new H0 line produced by Rivarossi was composed of five ready-to-run diesel and steam freight outfits. There were also separate three-unit diesels in popular and familiar Lionel train names such as Wabash, Illinois Central, Southern Pacific, Chicago & Northwestern, Western Pacific, and Texas & Pacific. They also produced two steam locomotive models, the 0610LT Consolidation and a small 0600 two-axle shunting locomotive, along with twenty pieces of freight-type rolling stock with authentic markings, some of which had never been seen previously in H0. It is interesting to note that Rivarossi's line for Lionel did not include any passenger rolling stock. What a beautiful set a Canadian Pacific passenger consist would have made in H0! Nevertheless, all the Rivarossi items were well made, handsome and highly detailed, particularly the boxcars which had such familiar markings as N.Y.C. Pacemaker, Seaboard, Rutland, Minneapolis & St. Louis, New Haven, Timken and B & O Sentinel.

The Lionel four-page H0 catalogue flyer also mentioned that the Lionel/Rivarossi motors were the only motors in the H0 field equipped with two sets of miniature steel thrust bearings, thus guaranteeing efficient performance and low friction. The catalogue proceeded to say that Lionel-Rivarossi motors were so precisely engineered and were so expertly designed electrically and mechanically that they would always run coolly while maintaining top efficiency with lower power drain. With sprung trucks, steel wheels, motors articulated and hinge-mounted to follow the motion of the power truck, hand-applied details—such as roofwalks, brakewheels, ladders and handrails, excellent paint application and graphics—and a one-year guarantee, authorized and backed by Lionel's extensive service station network, it seemed that Lionel was headed for success in H0. They had done almost everything right—even the package was a selling display in itself. Every component in

every outfit, as well as the outfit itself, peered from its own clear plastic window. Separate catalogues and promotional ads were sent to all dealers and vendors. It seemed that truly no efforts had been spared to make Lionel's entry into the H0 hobbyist market a successful one. As the **Railroad Model Craftsman** article, "Clear the Tracks for H0," stated in conclusion, "All of the above efforts by Lionel can only result in Lionel enhancing its position as the leader in American Model Railroading." Everything sounded so promising. The largest train manufacturer in America finally had entered the discriminating hobbyists' domain—here would be "H0 railroading at its very best!"[14] As the 1957 and 1958 Polk's Hobby Blue Books announced in a fictitious Western Union telegram, "Lionel announces H0 Gauge trains for 1957. H0 Gauge definitely has arrived with Lionel's recognition of this important adult hobbyist market."

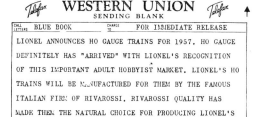

Announcement of Lionel H0 line from Polk's Hobby Blue Book.

It is interesting to note that it took Lionel's recognition to prove that H0 had finally "arrived." But, that was the kind of position Lionel held. In the model railroad industry, Lionel was number one, although 1957 was the last year in which the company showed a profit in electric trains.[15]

By 1958, something happened that caused an end to the honeymoon with Rivarossi, even though the excellent Rivarossi line sold well. According to Tom McComas' and Ron Hollander's research, Lionel discontinued its relationship with Rivarossi because the Italian company allegedly could not keep pace with the demand of Lionel and the American public for more trains.[16] That is certainly not the reason given by Rivarossi. In his letter of March 7, 1984, Il Presidente de Rivarossi states, "We supplied Lionel Corporation of N.Y. for the whole course of 1957 with our product, and the reason why our mutual business-trade suddenly ended was simply due to troubles arisen for payment questions. The first year, Messrs. Lionel opened a letter of credit as foreseen by our payment terms, but when, in 1958, they expected to affect payments by remittance, without any sort of bond or security, we have been compelled to state our refusal as we really couldn't accept such a condition. Messrs. Lionel Corp. did not find our sale-terms any longer suitable for their possibilities and therefore our trade inevitably broke off. That's all that we can say about our

---

12. Sam Belser, ibid.

13. **Railroad Model Craftsman**, pp. 53-54.

14. Lionel 1957 H0 catalog.

15. Hollander, p. 224.

16. McComas & Tuohy, ibid.

short business-ship with Messrs. Lionel, as due to time elapsed, no further correspondence or letters concerning this matter have been kept apart."[17]

The Rivarossi response sounds historically correct, because Lionel was beset with internal corporate problems by 1958. Joshua Lionel Cowen was semi-retired and living half the year in Palm Beach, Florida. Lionel seemed to have lost its direction and focus. Remember that the now-famous 0 Gauge Girls' Train was also being marketed in 1957 and unloaded in 1958. There is speculation that a girls' train was contemplated in H0 as well (one author has acquired a Rivarossi boxcar "paint sample" collection and a similar robin's-egg blue boxcar with yellow door was found in H0. It matches the 0 Gauge counterpart), but the conjecture is that the H0 scale set could not be justified because of the miserable failure of the 0 Gauge project.

On December 18, 1958, Joshua Lionel Cowen retired, and in September, 1959, he sold his shares of Lionel stock.[18] Sales in electric trains dropped from $18.7 million in 1957 to $14.4 million by the end of 1958.[19] The company showed a loss of $469,000, its first losing year since the Depression. By October of 1959, Lawrence Cowen too was bought out by the Roy Cohn group (Cowen's great nephew).[20]

In the midst of all this confusion, Lionel decided to expand their H0 line for 1958 and turned to Athearn, an American company which they felt already had an established domestic following. Athearn also produced an excellent quality train, but its motor drive system (with rubber belt transmission) could not compare with Rivarossi's gear drive and steel bearings. The Athearn rolling stock, diesels and rectifiers looked like miniature Lionels, but it may have been a major mistake to introduce the lower quality, unreliable belt-driven locomotives and diesels to the quality-conscious H0 hobbyists that Lionel so desperately wanted to reach back in 1957. One of the beautiful aspects of H0 is that the locomotives can creep at prototypical speeds. This was hard to achieve with the Athearn locomotives. Nevertheless, a deal was made with Irv Athearn which, we suspect, included Lionel's terms for down payment and remittance. The Athearn line was cheaper to sell. For example, an 0864-50 Rivarossi boxcar in State of Maine livery was $3.75 in 1957. The same boxcar by Athearn sold for $2.50.

The connection with Athearn did give Lionel an interim period for development of its own style of H0, but the Athearn connection, too, was short lived. It lasted from 1958 to 1960, when Lionel began to produce the H0 line in its factory in Hillside, New Jersey.

Three versions of the colorful State of Maine boxcar. The Rivarossi model shown on the top shelf has separate ladders added to the body shell, while the Athearn model on the second shelf and the model manufactured by Lionel at the bottom have ladders molded onto the body casting. Unlike the other two, the Lionel version has its roofwalk molded onto the body shell.

17. Letter from Rivarossi President Alessandro Rossi to Vincent Rosa, March 7, 1984.

18. Ibid, p. 230.

19. McComas & Tuohy, p. 105.

20. Hollander, p. 232.

Chapter II
Lionel/Rivarossi Trains

0610 Light Consolidation

TRENI ELECTRICI IN MINATURA
INTRODUCTION

In 1957, when Lionel entered the H0 market, all of its H0 products were manufactured by Rivarossi of Italy. Rivarossi was then almost unknown in the U.S., as very few dealers carried their products, which included individual model kits as well as complete, ready-to-run train sets that sold in the $25.00 range. Even then the models were superior in workmanship. All had frames of cast metal, sheet metal or occasionally brass. The body shells were molded very solidly with an extra-heavy type of plastic, and the mechanisms used excellent motors. Rivarossi identified the products that it sold in the United States, which were compatible with American-made models, with its Red Line label. Today, all of these, including those produced on behalf of Lionel Corporation, are rare and desirable to the H0 collector. For Rivarossi, the brief engagement with Lionel provided additional exposure of its line to the large American market.

Presently, Rivarossi enjoys a fair share of the U. S. market. The company produces not only trains in H0 and other popular scales, but also trackside and electrical accessories as well. Furthermore, Rivarossi's market includes countries across Europe and other continents. One wonders what might have happened if, in 1957, Lionel had made an investment in the production capability of Rivarossi.

PLASTICS

In describing certain variations in the production of Rivarossi models, it is necessary to distinguish between phenolic plastics and thermoplastics. Reader Lou Bohn, a professional engineer, has offered the following information.

Phenolic plastics, of which Bakelite is just one brand, are thermosetting plastics which cannot be heated and remelted once molded. These plastics withstand higher temperatures without deforming. The phenolics are brown, dark brown and black in color, and they are always opaque. Commonly used in electrical insulation and normally found in relatively thick sections. Bakelite is brittle, so thin sections are easily broken.

Thermoplastics, on the other hand, can be heated, softened and remelted. They withstand a lower operating temperature before deformation occurs. With plasticizer, these can be "softened" so that they will not crack as easily. Most plastic model train bodies are made of polystyrene with varied amounts of plasticizer added to make them less brittle. The plasticizer dessicates in time, and thus the body cracks around screw mounting holes. This class of plastics is also available without pigmentation (clear). It yellows in time due to ultraviolet degradation. Very fine molding detail is possible, as are heat-stamped graphics.

STEAM LOCOMOTIVES

Lionel's first H0 catalogue, a four-page color folder, showed a 4-4-2 Atlantic locomotive on its cover. This particular locomotive was sold in the early 1960s under the Aristo Craft trade name, but never under the Lionel name. The Atlantic locomotive and the two that were sold as Lionel, in 1957, were originally marketed in the U.S.A. in 1955 under the name Rivarossi "Red Line." The information on the two sold under Lionel's name follows.

Gd Exc Mt

0600 Dockside Switcher

0600 B&O-type dockside switcher; black, painted plastic body; unlettered; cast steam chest; brass bell; wire handrails at the cab doors, boiler front and

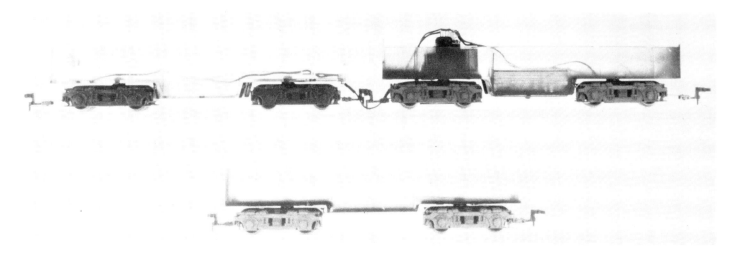

The typical Rivarossi F.M. diesel frame is made of clear plastic, which appears as window glazing in the side portholes.

along the length of the boiler sides; full working valve gear; drivers are steel tires with plastic centers, the same type used on the 0610 Consolidation; lighted. A 3/4" cast weight is located at the front of the boiler, ending at the center of the first driver. The size of this weight can help differentiate the Lionel locomotive from those imported in the 1960s. The later locomotives have a much larger weight that extends to a point just in front of the second driver. "1050" and "R.R. Italy" appear on the plastic section of the frame; "Rivarossi", "COMO, Italy" and "1051" appear directly below the motor. The rear of the motor housing is constructed of heavy white plastic; post-1958 models have black Bakelite instead. In 1956 this particular locomotive was sold in the Rivarossi packaging and identified on the carton as 1018. In 1960 A.H.M. also imported this same locomotive with some small changes in boiler detail. They are all very much alike with few small changes. The Rivarossi builder's plate appears on all versions. The boiler must be removed to replace the light bulb. Catalogued in 1957 at $12.95 as a separate item and also with one three-car set, number 5700, which sold for $25.00. Lionel's 0600 is quite difficult to find.　**20　35　60**

0610 Light Consolidation (2-8-0); black plastic cab and boiler; European-type, arched windows; wire handrails on boiler front, pilot and length of boiler; steel driver rims with plastic centers; sheet metal frame; cast metal pilot truck; larger metal weight in boiler; headlight located behind removable boiler front; turned brass bell; three pop-off valves; the Rivarossi signature, "COMO, Italy" and "1515" appear under the cab on the bottom of the frame. Two small jumper wires, as found on multiple-unit diesels, connect the locomotive and tender for electrical pickup, while a metal drawbar, attached with a screw at either end, provides a mechanical connection. The tender houses the motor, the power of which is transmitted to the locomotive gear box by means of a flexible shaft. Plastic tender body, lettered "280" in heavy white printing, although this is not shown in the catalogue; wire handrails at the cab end; cast metal tender frame, with lettering matching that on the locomotive frame. The arched cab windows help to distinguish the locomotive from Rivarossi Consolidations sold by other firms. Later, non-Lionel versions feature rectangular windows and different types of coal piles. Lionel's model was catalogued in 1957 as a

separate item for $33.50; it also headed one freight set, number 5704, with six cars, which sold for $49.95. It carried no Lionel numbers or logos on the cab, however the number did appear on the carton. It is possible that the tender was available as described with the exception of a sheet metal frame; verification of this variation is requested.

(A) Painted body.　**30　70　120**
(B) Unpainted body.　**30　70　120**

FAIRBANKS-MORSE DIESELS

FRAMES AND MOTORS

The following information can be used to identify all Rivarossi Diesel F.M. units catalogued as Lionel in 1957 with the exception of the few brass frame models known to exist. All powered A units are equipped with hinge-mounted, articulated, gear-driven rear power trucks. All trucks have machined steel wheels with good electrical contact; all wheels are flanged, and two are equipped with rubber tires. They are good performers with good pulling power. The body has one-piece plastic construction with excellent rivet detail. The Rivarossi signature, the words "COMO Italy" and the mold number 305 appear on the inside roof of each power unit. The units have no steps or ladders except on the pilot. The steps on the pilot help to distinguish Lionel units from models sold under the A.H.M. label in the 1960s. The frame of each unit is molded in clear plastic, with the floor being painted black. The inch-high, clear sides served as side reinforcement and as lenses for the number boards and headlights and as window glass for the doors of the unit. There is no window material in the cab itself. In the A unit a large lead weight is located at the very rear of the frame, and another weight made of ten or so

Rare version of the F.M. diesel frame. It was used on Rivarossi Red Line models, 1950-1954, and appeared on a few of the earliest Lionel models.

This apparently occurred due to Lionel's rush to enter the market.

thin metal plates rests in the middle of the frame just in front of the motor. These plates are riveted in place. The truck frames are plastic, with metal axle covers holding each axle in place. All units carry N.M.R.A.-type couplers at both ends. Each powered A and dummy A is lighted with one screw-base bulb, which is easily replaced. The body is fastened to the frame by four tabs built into the frame. They fit snugly into receiving holes in the side of each body. There are also two metal sockets on either side of the frame at the rear of each unit. These sockets accept small electrical jumper wires that transmit the power from the powered A through the B and into the dummy A for lighting purposes only. The dummy B unit has much the same construction, with only minor changes. Trucks are bolted in place, and there are four electric sockets, one in each corner of the frame. With the exception of the rear power truck on the A unit, all trucks are fastened with a nut and bolt. The wire from one end to the other is bare of insulation. The Rivarossi signature and "COMO, Italy" are also in the roof of these units and the mold number is 1373. The B unit also has the painted black floor with clear sides. The B unit carries no weights and thus derails easily. The body fastens to the frame in the same manner as that of the powered A. Dummy A units are the same as powered A units with the exception of the weights; dummy A units carry none and also derail easily. There is a screw-base bulb at the front of the cab and the same two electric sockets. It has no electrical pickup of its own. Since no weights are riveted in the center of this unit, the Rivarossi name is visible on the outside frame without having to remove the shell. **NOTE:** The wire handrails shown clearly in the 1957 catalogue did not appear on any F.M. unit with the exception of the two small rails on the nose of each A unit. This, it seems, is the reason why most units will be found with nose decals intact. All units did carry cast-on handrails at all door openings.

A RARE F.M. VARIATION

The frames on the earliest F.M. units are sheet brass, painted flat black, with a cast metal weight riveted to the center. Fixed between the frame and weight is a strip of spring steel bent outward. The ends snap into the holes in the side of the shell to secure it to the frame. The frame itself has at its end two tabs that slide into holes in the rear of the shell. The jacks for the jumper wires are also present, but there is no window material. The front truck is bolted in place, and there is a solder joint for lighting purposes. The frame is actually a continuation from the early locomotive sold in the U.S. under the Red Line name, which again shows the rush Lionel made to enter the H0 market. The shell itself is made of Bakelite rather than polstyrene, as found on most other models. This appears to be the first type of the locomotive sold under the Lionel name. One co-author has one A unit with W.P. markings and has seen B units in W.P. and Wabash markings. All carry the Lionel logo but no Lionel numbers are used. All other information listed on the F.M. units applies here, with the exception of truck side frames which are cast metal. Very rare.

PROTOTYPE NOTE: The Rivarossi diesels are models of Fairbanks Morse Company C-Liners. The Fairbanks Morse Company was famous for its World War II submarine diesels. These diesels had an unusual design with opposed pistons. This apparently increased the amount of power available for a given volume. F.M. recognized that its diesel motor could be applied to locomotives. Eventually they offered three lines: 1600, 2000 and 2400 horsepower engines.

A comparison of the shells from two Rivarossi F.M. units. The earlier unit, on the left, has two slots for frame tabs beneath the back door. The later unit does not have the slots.

Note: These models are grouped in A-B-A sets for each road name. All F.M. units listed as carrying the Lionel logo on their sides have the larger 1/8" diameter logo.

0500 CHICAGO & NORTHWESTERN Powered A unit; battery boxes, pilot, top row of side panels and roof painted green; yellow lower side panels and nose; black pin stripes separate colors; road name spelled out in reddish-orange lettering on the lower yellow side panels; wire handrails and the C.N.W. winged decal herald appear on the nose; another logo decal appears under the first cab window; lighted; two decorative horns on roof; green, painted plastic truck side frames; no number on unit; catalogue number appears on carton; catalogued in 1957, as a separate unit at $15.95 or in A-B-A sets at $27.85; not catalogued in any set; very rare and prized.

(A) With Lionel logo.	45	90	120
(B) Without Lionel logo.	45	90	120

0520 CHICAGO & NORTHWESTERN Dummy B unit; painted to match the powered A unit; road name spread from door to door in the lower side panels; not lighted; no Lionel logo; no number on unit; catalogue number appears on the carton; catalogued in 1957 separately at $4.95 and as part of an A-B-A set; very rare and highly prized.　　　50　　70　　120

0510 CHICAGO & NORTHWESTERN Dummy A unit; painted exactly as powered A unit; lighted; no Lionel logo; catalogued in 1957 as a separate item at $6.95 and in an A-B-A set at $27.85; not catalogued in any set; very rare and highly prized.　　　50　　70　　120

0501 TEXAS & PACIFIC Powered A unit; very pale, painted bluish-gray body; flat white roof, pilot, battery boxes and middle row of side panels; dark gray truck side frames; road name printed on two card stock panels, glued to the top side panels; yellow "TP" winged herald decal on nose, just under headlight; wire grab-irons; two black decorative horns; lighted; catalogue number appears on carton only; catalogued in 1957 as a separate item and in an A-B-A set; very rare.

(A) With Lionel logo.	70	80	100
(B) Without Lionel logo.	70	80	100

0521 TEXAS & PACIFIC Dummy B unit; painted to match powered A unit; road name appears on card stock panels on top row of side panels; no light; catalogue number appears on carton; catalogued in 1957 as a separate unit and in A-B-A combinations only; very rare.　　50　　60　　70

0511 TEXAS & PACIFIC Dummy A unit; painted and decorated with decals exactly the same as powered A unit; lighted; catalogue number appears on carton in 1957 as separate unit and in an A-B-A combination; very rare.　　　40　　60　　70

0502 WABASH Powered A unit; dark blue, painted body; light gray rear of unit, roof, nose and top row of side panels; white band on lower side panels from just behind the front cab door to the rear of unit; 1/8" white

0500   0520   0510

0504   0524   0514

0501   0521   0511

0505   0525   0515

0502   0522   0512

0503(B)   0523(B)   0513(B)

0503(C)   0523(A)   0513(A)

No Number   No Number

A beautiful array of Rivarossi Fairbanks-Morse C-Liners built for Lionel in 1957. The F.M. units are very nicely detailed and both the powered A and dummy A unit in each set are lighted; the jumper wires between the units provide current for lighting in the dummy. While the F.M. units do not have numbers on the sides, the collector can readily identify models by finding the correct road name listing in the text.

The two shelves of Western Pacific models illustrate subtle differences in appearance. The models on the higher shelf have plastic frames with window glazing and plastic bodies. Note that the dummy at right has black trucks — a factory error collected in original box. The models on the lower shelf have the earlier sheet metal frames, without window glazing, and Bakelite bodies. The Santa Fe units on the bottom shelves are preproduction samples without lettering. Decorated at the Lionel factory, these prototypes were acquired in original boxes with "0000" decals applied on the end. The Santa Fe scheme was never produced on the Lionel/Rivarossi models.

0864-150   0864-50(A)   0864-50(B)

0864-175   0864-125   0864-75

0866   0864-25   0864-100

0872-25   0872-50   0872-1

0862-1   0864-1   0862-25

Rivarossi produced very attractive, well-detailed rolling stock for Lionel. Both variations of the State of Maine boxcar are shown; note the potato decal that appears to the left of the door on the rarer variety. The M-K-T stock car shown on the third shelf and the Seaboard outside-braced boxcar shown at bottom center represent the only road names for those particular car types.

stripe above the white band from just in front of the rear cab door to the rear of the unit; road name and Lionel logo appear in gold, silk-screened lettering on the second and third panel in the white band; two wire handrails and the Wabash flag appear on the nose; excellent rivet detail; black plastic truck side frames; two black plastic decorative air horns; lighted; catalogue number appears on the carton; no number on unit itself; catalogued in 1957 as a separate item at $15.95, in an A-B-A set at $27.85 and in set 5702 with five cars at $39.95.   **40 50 90**

0522 WABASH Dummy B unit; painted to match A unit; gray ends; white striping along the full length of unit; road name and Lionel logo appear in the fourth and fifth white side panels; no other detail, number or light; catalogue number appears on the carton; catalogued in 1957 in set 5702, as a separate item and in an A-B-A set.
(A) Bakelite body; sheet brass frame; rare.   **NRS**
(B) Polystyrene plastic body; standard frame.   **20 30 40**

0512 WABASH Dummy A unit; all information regarding the powered A applies here, with the exception of the weights; no number on unit; catalogue number appears on carton; catalogued in 1957 as a separate unit and in an A-B-A set. This road name is somewhat common, thus variation (B) is fairly plentiful in the lower grades.
(A) Bakelite body; sheet brass frame; rare.   **NRS**
(B) Polystyrene plastic body; standard frame.   **25 35 70**

0503 WESTERN PACIFIC Powered A unit; body and truck side frames painted light, semi-gloss gray; nose of unit, from below the windshield to the top of the pilot and the middle row of side panels, is deep orange; winged herald decal appears on nose just below headlight; wire handrails on nose; road name, in crisp black lettering, appears on the lower gray side panels; Lionel logo, also in black, also appears in these panels in front of the rear door; lighted; two black decorative horns on the roof; no number on unit; catalogued in 1957 as a separate unit at $15.95, in an A-B-A set and

in a five-car set, 5703, with A-B-A locomotives, at $45.00; scarce but obtainable.
(A) Light gray truck side frames.   **45 60 70**
(B) Dark gray truck side frames.   **45 60 70**

0523 WESTERN PACIFIC Dummy B unit; painted to match exactly the A unit; road name and Lionel logo appear in black lettering on the gray side panels; no light; no number; catalogue number appears on carton; catalogued in 1957 separately at $4.95, in an A-B-A set and with set 5703 at $45.00; scarce.   **30 40 45**

0513 WESTERN PACIFIC Dummy A unit; description of powered unit applies here.
(A) Bakelite body; sheet metal frame; rare.   **NRS**
(B) Polystyrene plastic body; standard frame; scarce.   **30 50 60**

0504 SOUTHERN PACIFIC Powered A unit; painted deep red; 1/2" wide light gray stripe begins at the handrails on the nose and covers the bottom row of side panels and battery boxes; "Southern Pacific" decal under the headlight, protected by the wire handrails; road name printed in black letters on two gray card stock boards, which are glued in place on the top row of side panels; stamped lettering; two black decorative horns; lighted; no number; darker gray truck side frames; catalogued in 1957 as a separate unit at $15.95 and in an A-B-A set. It is shown in the catalogue with black truck side frames, but they are found only in painted gray; very rare and highly prized.
(A) With Lionel logo.   **50 70 100**
(B) Without Lionel logo.   **50 70 100**

0524 SOUTHERN PACIFIC Dummy B unit; painted to match exactly the A unit; lettering appears on two card stock letterboards, as found on A unit; no light; no Lionel logo; catalogue number appears on carton; catalogued in 1957 at $4.95 and in A-B-A sets; very rare and highly prized.   **40 50 60**

Underside of a Rivarossi boxcar. Note presence of talgo-type trucks and absence of added detail parts.

0514 SOUTHERN PACIFIC Dummy A unit; all information regarding description of powered A unit applies here; catalogued in 1957 as a separate unit at $6.95 and in A-B-A sets; very rare and highly prized.

(A) With Lionel logo.	40	50	60
(B) Without Lionel logo.	40	50	60

0505 ILLINOIS CENTRAL Powered A unit; light brown, painted body; 1/2" orange band on the lower side panels and nose; two yellow pin stripes separate the band from the floor and the brown portion of body; road name appears in brown lettering; black truck side frames, pilot and battery boxes; no numbers; green I.C. logo decal appears on the nose, with wire handrails on either side; Lionel logo, also in brown, appears in the second orange side panel from the rear of the units; two black decorative horns on the roof; lighted; catalogue number appears on carton; catalogued in 1957 as a separate unit, in A-B-A sets and at the head of set 5701 with five cars at $29.00; scarce.   **40   50   75**

0525 ILLINOIS CENTRAL Dummy B unit; matches A unit, except orange band appears only on side panels; brown ends; no light; Lionel logo situated as described for A unit; no number on unit; catalogue number appears on carton; catalogued in 1957 as a separate unit at $4.95 and in an A-B-A combination; scarce.   **30   60   70**

0515 ILLINOIS CENTRAL Dummy A unit; matches description of powered A unit; catalogue number appears on carton; catalogued in 1957 as a separate unit and in an A-B-A combination; very rare.   **40   55   80**

BOXCARS

The boxcars sold in 1957 by Lionel were fine looking models precisely engineered by Rivarossi of Italy, and they are among the scarcest of Lionel HO items. There are a total of eight different boxcars. With the exception of the 0864-1 Seaboard boxcar, all of the cars are standard 40-foot steel-type cars. All have metal door runners, sprung trucks, roofwalks (almost always matching the painted roof), plastic ladders, with N.M.R.A.-type couplers, crisp silk-screened lettering and fine rivet detail. They are assembled of plastic parts. None are weighted for operation. The catalogue clearly shows under-the-floor detail, but none came with any car sold by Lionel. The eighth car, the Seaboard boxcar, reproduced a 40-foot wooden boxcar with outside bracing, and it carries all of the other detail previously mentioned.

None of the cars carry a Lionel catalogue number, but all of them have the Lionel logo, which appears in three different diameters on the car sides. The logo varies in diameter from 1/16 inch to just over 1/8 inch in size. Another interesting distinction between Lionel and Rivarossi are floors. Rivarossi floors have detail, the words "COMO, Italia Made in Italy" and the Rivarossi signature on the outside of the floor. The Lionel floor carries no detail parts, although there are cast-on receptacles to accept the valves, brake cylinders and reservoir. The words "COMO Italia", mold number "1228" and the Rivarossi name in print also appear on the floor, but there is no signature. There are also coupler pockets cast into the floors of both Lionel and non-Lionel cars. These pockets are not used on the Lionel cars, as they are equipped with the talgo trucks and couplers. It is believed that the State of Maine, B&0, Timken, Pacemaker and Rutland boxcars are the only cars made exclusively for the Lionel Corporation. The other three road names were sold in the Rivarossi line before 1957 and can be found that way, with the exception of the Lionel logo and outside frame detail. The cars sold for $3.75 each in 1957, but range in value now from $25.00 to $100.00 depending on condition. All are most difficult to find and much sought after by HO collectors. Lionel's catalogue number does appear on the cartons.

0864-1 SEABOARD Painted tuscan body; white lettering; "15412" to the left of door, under road name; 1/8" diameter Lionel logo appears to the right of door, in the last panel "LIONEL"; catalogue number appears on carton; catalogued 1957; catalogued again in 1958, without illustration; rare. This car is the only wooden-type boxcar offered in the Lionel HO line.   **70   80   100**

0864-25 NEW YORK CENTRAL "PACEMAKER" Painted gray and red; solid red door; white lettering; 1/16" diameter Lionel logo appears on the fourth gray panel to the left of the door; "174478" on car side; catalogued in 1957 and shown without steps, although steps are found on car; catalogued also in 1958, during Athearn's production, but no longer available then.   **30   40   90**

0864-50 STATE OF MAINE Painted in the well-known red, white and blue paint scheme; black door guides and ladders; blue and white lettering; 1/16" diameter Lionel logo on red portion of the third side panel to the right of the door; red, white and blue door; blue roof and roofwalk; blue "2300" to the left of door; the car does have steps, although none are shown in the catalogue. By 1958, Athearn was making Lionel HO, but the Rivarossi car was still depicted in the catalogue.

(A) Extremely rare variation with a decal showing a pototo on the white panel to the left of the door.   **NRS**

(B) No potato decal.   **25   40   70**

0864-75 B&O SENTINEL Beautifully painted in the silver and blue Sentinel colors with matching striped door; one of three boxcars to carry a decal; "Sentinel Service" logo appears on a bright yellow decal to the right of the door; a white, 1/8" diameter Lionel logo appears next to the ladder and just below the decal; "466464" on car side; catalogued for only one year, 1957; very difficult to find in good condition.   **40   60   95**

0864-100 NEW HAVEN Black; orange door; large, white lettering; "36409" at right of door; Lionel logo appears to the right of the door in the second panel; catalogue number appears on carton; catalogued in 1957-58.

(A) Dull, painted black body; solid orange, painted door; large Lionel logo.   **30   50   70**

(B) Similar to (A), except smaller logo; sometimes this logo is hidden by the door guide.   **30   50   70**

(C) Unpainted, glossy black body; solid orange, unpainted door; large Lionel logo.   **30   50   70**

(D) Similar to (C), except smaller logo.   **30   50   70**

0864-125 RUTLAND Painted yellow and green body; solid yellow door; darker green lettering on yellow portion of side; small Lionel logo appears on the fourth green panel to the right of door; small "104" to the left of door; with steps; catalogued in 1957-58 and shown without steps. The color of the car as shown in the two catalogues is quite different, but it was the Rivarossi car pictured in 1958. There is some question whether Athearn may have made this car in 1958-59; neither author has seen such a car.

40   60   75

0864-150 MINNEAPOLIS & ST. LOUIS Bright red; heavyweight lettering; "54652" in the second and third panel to the left of the door; unpainted, black plastic door, roofwalk and ladders; Lionel logo appears in the second panel to the right of the door. The car has steps, though none were shown in the catalogue; catalogued in 1957. This boxcar and the following N.Y.C. Pacemaker cars were the only boxcars lettered with only a road name, number and herald. The lack of other markings gave these cars a very plain appearance. In 1958, Athearn reproduced this car with the same catalogue number; the Athearn car appeared in set 5709, and it is described in the Athearn section of the text.

(A) Painted body; small Lionel logo, less than 1/16" diameter.

30   35   65

(B) Unpainted body; larger, 1/8" diameter logo.   **30   35   65**

0864-175 TIMKEN Painted bright yellow; 1/2" wide white band on side and door; black and dark blue lettering; third car to have a decal; "Roller Freight" on a red and white decal to the right of the door; 1/16" diameter Lionel logo appears just below the decal in the fourth panel; "6464-50" appears to the left of the door; catalogued in 1957; also pictured in 1958 and 1959, during Athearn production years. The Timken and B & O Sentinel cars are the only boxcars that come close to carrying a Lionel catalogue number on the car side.   **30   40   70**

REFRIGERATOR CARS

Because Rivarossi produced trains for Lionel for only one year, it is difficult to locate the three reefer cars and one stock car carried in the 1957 line. The information regarding trucks, couplers and construction, which was used to identify the boxcars, applies to reefers. The floor, trucks and printing on the floor are exactly the same. Of course, the colors, the road names and the car numbers differ. All of the lettering is silk-screened.

0872-1 FRUIT GROWERS EXPRESS Bright yellow, painted sides; tuscan ends, roof and roofwalk; black plastic brakewheel and ladder; heavy black lettering; 1/8" diameter Lionel logo appears in the last panel to the right of the door; doors do not open, but the handle and hinges are raised and outlined in black, thus giving the appearance of operability; "39783" on car side; catalogued in 1957-58 only; very difficult to find.   **25   40   70**

0872-25 ILLINOIS CENTRAL Bright silver, painted body and roofwalk; deep, glossy green lettering, including road name, herald and car number "51604"; thin green pin stripes along sill; 1/8" diameter Lionel logo appears in the last panel to the right of the door; catalogued in 1957-58 at $2.95 and $2.50, respectively; this car has an outstanding appearance, and it would certainly delight any collector to find it at or near the original price.

30   45   80

0872-50 A.T.S.F. EL CAPITAN Dark orange, painted sides; black roof, roofwalk and ends; heavy black lettering; "El Capitan" slogan on one side of car, "Ship and Travel" slogan on other; black and white Santa Fe cross herald located in the fourth panel to the left of door; "8175" appears directly below herald; 1/8" diameter Lionel logo located in the last side panel to the right of the door; door and hinges outlined in raised black; separate brakewheel and ladders; catalogued in 1957; Rivarossi car shown

again in 1958 catalogue, although Athearn had assumed production; illustration shows no steps.   **20   35   60**

STOCK CARS

The M.K.T. Cattle car is the only cattle car that Lionel sold in 1957. Although some other companies marketed much the same car, even down to the same number, it is nevertheless a desirable piece for the H0 collector and as difficult to find as the other Rivarossi pieces.

0866 M.K.T. Bright yellow, painted sides and ends; tuscan roof and roofwalk; black lettering; unpainted black plastic brakewheel and plastic ladders; working door with steel guides; "The Katy" on letterboard at one side of door; "502" on letterboard on opposite side of door; black Lionel logo appears at floor line in the third panel to the left of the door; catalogued in 1957-58 at $3.25 and $2.50, respectively; Rivarossi car illustrated in 1958; steps shown. The Lionel logo is the only difference between this car and those sold under different brand names.   **10   25   40**

GONDOLAS

Returning to the cover of the 1957 catalogue folder, we can plainly see a yellow gondola, but there were no yellow gondolas sold that year. There were only two gondolas available in 1957; both were the 40-foot cars. There were changes in the mold used on these cars, which have one-piece plastic construction. There are only five floor braces. The fine rivet detail remains, as does the cast-on receptacle to receive the valves, reservoir, etc. These receptacles are much thicker than those found on any other car. Again, no detail parts came with the cars. The steps were much heavier than those used on the boxcars. The underside of the cars read "Made in Italy" and "Rivarossi". The same trucks and couplers used on the boxcars are found on the gondolas. Both cars were molded in colored plastic, with each shell being the same color as it would be painted.

0862-1 PENNSYLVANIA Tuscan red, painted body; heavy white lettering; PRR herald; Lionel logo appears in the center of the last panel, just above the floor line; separate brakewheel; numbered "357843"; no load; catalogued in 1957 only at $2.25.   **10   20   25**

0862-25 MICHIGAN CENTRAL Flat black, painted body; white, stamped lettering; "M.C.R.R."; Lionel logo appears in the last side panel; numbered "15317"; no load; catalogued in 1957 only, at $2.25. This particular car has lettering in seven of eight side panels, thus having a very crowded appearance; it is also the only car not having silk-screened lettering.

8   10   15

FLATS, MISCELLANEOUS CARS & CABOOSES

These cars are grouped together because these are all based on the same design, made from the same mold and differ only in the type of car they eventually became. Each car is molded in plastic of the same color the car is painted; however, the undersides are not painted. The cast-on steps are lighter and much smaller in width and length than those found on the boxcars. "Made in Italy" and "Rivarossi" also appear on these cars, but in much smaller lettering. The mold number, too, appears, as do the receptacles for the brake and valve, but once again no detail came with the cars. The red Reading and the black Illinois Central car body, no matter how they were used, were the only two cars in the entire line that did not have a road name spelled out on their sides. Toward the end of 1957

0877(B)   0877(A)   0811-25

0811-1   0860   0819

0811(B)   0811(A)   0857

All of the freight cars illustrated in this photograph bear the circular Lionel logo. The bulkhead flatcar with load is an uncatalogued item from 1957. The flatcar shown on the left of the third shelf has a peculiar mounting fixture which may have been intended for a load that never appeared on the car. Note that the road numbers present on Rivarossi freight cars do not correspond to the Lionel catalogue numbers.

The Milwaukee Road Hiawatha locomotive is a Rivarossi model that Lionel did not sell. Lionel did offer an 0 Gauge model of this locomotive (number 250E in the Prewar line), so it may surprise some that the company did not import the H0 model. However, one expert has indicated that the 0 Gauge model did not sell well, and that this experience proscribed the introduction of the smaller version.

Most of these models are Rivarossi shells that were painted by Lionel when new road names were being considered. The crane is made from styrene plastic; it was never produced. The center car could be either a Boston & Maine prototype, which was later produced by Rivarossi. Or, if we wish to believe that Lionel considered producing an H0 version of its Girls' train set, it could be a sample for that item. Since the 0 Gauge Girls' set failed, the H0 set, if considered at all, would have been dropped from production plans. The green outside-braced boxcar is the same type as the brown Seaboard boxcar.

The brown and white boxcar on the second shelf appears to be a mock-up for a Monon paint scheme, while the green car could have been lettered for many different road names. The caboose at right is a Varney shell acquired in a Lionel box stamped "prototype." Apparently, a bay window caboose was considered for the H0 line.

some of these cars appeared as uncatalogued items. We attribute this fact to Rivarossi's knowledge that they would soon lose their contract to supply Lionel, their biggest American buyer. It was less expensive for them to add sidewalls, stakes and pipe loads from their own line of cars to the cars made for Lionel and to ship them as uncatalogued items. These uncatalogued cars are all highly prized.

Although an eight-wheel red caboose with Lionel lettering appears on the cover of the 1957 catalogue, this type of car was neither made nor sold by Lionel in 1957. The Bobber Caboose, like the Seaboard Boxcar, never appeared in the catalogue after 1957. Strange as it may seem, there were six road names used on the diesel units in 1957, but only two road names used on cabooses. Neither matches a locomotive road name. This oversight, like the others, can be attributed to Lionel's hasty entry into the H0 market.

0811 ILLINOIS CENTRAL Flatcar; "uncatalogued"; standard flatcar also used as 0877 miscellaneous car; black, painted body; white lettering, with the initials "I.C." and the number "63234"; Lionel logo appears to the right of the lettering; standing brakewheel; "0811" appears on the carton; the liner of the carton points to the fact that there was no load with the car; first appeared at the end of 1957; extremely rare.
(A) 1/8" high sidewalls the length of the car; four pockets to accept a truck trailer. **10   16   20**
(B) Black plastic mounting platform with square base and round top held on the car with four steel stakes; this platform may have been intended for some other load never actually made for the car. **10   16   20**

0811-1 PENNSYLVANIA Flatcar; light gray, painted body; "PENNSYL-VANIA" in heavy black lettering; black Lionel logo appears in the neighboring side panel; no additional lettering; twelve black plastic stakes; floor has four pre-drilled holes to accept the work caboose cab, which is used with this same flatcar body to produce the gray work caboose; catalogued in 1957 only, at $2.25; hard to find with the stakes. **15   25   40**

0811-25 READING Flatcar; bright red, painted body; heavy white lettering, with "R.D.G." initials; numbered "91306"; Lionel logo appears in the third side panel on the right side of the car; separate brakewheel and twelve black plastic stakes; no load; catalogued 1957-58, at $2.25; very rare in mint condition. **15   25   40**

0819 PENNSYLVANIA WORK CABOOSE Painted gray; black lettering; road name, herald, Lionel logo and "6475" appear on car side; separate brakewheel, ladder, grab-irons and smokestack in black; marker lights cast onto the end of the cab; same body used on the 0811-1 gray flatcar; catalogue number appears on carton; catalogued in 1957 only. **24   30   40**

0857 RED BOBBER-TYPE CABOOSE Red, painted body; unpainted, black plastic and metal frame; white lettering; "READING", "90258" and the Lionel logo appear on side; wire handrails; separate ladders at each end, brakewheel and smokestack; cast-on marker lights; mold number "1118", "Rivarossi" and "COMO, Italy" appear at one end of the plastic frame; this is the only car with body-mounted couplers, although the pockets are cast into the floor of every Rivarossi car; catalogue number appears on carton; catalogued in 1957. **24   30   65**

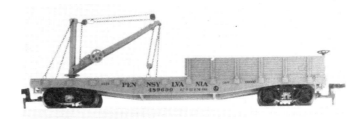

0860 Pennsylvania Crane Car

0860 PENNSYLVANIA CRANE CAR Painted gray; heavy black lettering; Lionel logo and "489690" on side; no toolboxes; plastic side fences run half the length of the car, opposite the crane end; highly-detailed crane, with cranks, cogs and hooks; fine chain from the top of the boom and back to the floor, secured in place with small wire eyelets; catalogue number appears on carton; catalogued in 1957-58, at $4.25; because of the delicate detail on the car, it is most difficult to find with the boom unbroken and the chain intact. **25   40   60**

0877 BLACK I.C. MISCELLANEOUS CAR With the exception of the bulkhead ends added to the car, it is exactly the same as the black 0811; separate brakewheel; catalogue number does not appear on carton; catalogued in 1957 at $2.50 without a load.
(A) Early 1957, no load. **16   24   30**
(B) Late 1957; three silver metal pipes held in place with four steel stakes and a yellow rubber band; extremely rare with load intact. **NRS**

Chapter III
Athearn to the Rescue:
H0 in 1958

Athearn, Incorporated, one of the oldest manufacturers of H0 equipment, is also one of the most respected names in H0 model railroading. The company produces an extensive line of models sold under its own name and supplies smaller firms with locomotives and rolling stock for various custom-painting projects, such as fund raisers for clubs and limited editions featuring less common road names.

If we assume that Lionel wished to engage a competent subcontractor for the production of its H0 scale line, then we should not be surprised that they chose Athearn. Only a few years prior to Lionel's entry into the H0 market, Athearn had begun to produce injection-molded plastic models. With the rapid acceptance and economies of scale associated with the production of plastic kits, Athearn grew quickly. At the same time Lionel was terminating its relationship with Rivarossi, Athearn was expanding into six facilities and enlarging its staff to approximately three hundred. In 1956 Athearn designated certain of its production facilities for the assembly of kits; by Christmas Athearn had begun to produce ready-to-run train sets. Almost literally, Athearn shocked the market with its very low prices. Whether Lionel officials searched widely or not, they certainly would have found this: Athearn produced good-quality H0 models very efficiently.

President Irvin Athearn recalls that Lionel officials invited him to New York to discuss the feasibility of a contractual relationship.[1] However, no agreement was made during Athearn's trip. In fact, Athearn claims that he went back to Los Angeles and "forgot about it" before Lionel made its response. In considering the terms set forth by Athearn, Lionel had to evaluate many considerations. First, it had to decide whether its entry into the H0 market should be a permanent or a temporary commitment. Had Lionel decided to make it a permanent commitment at the outset or immediately after the Rivarossi relationship, the company might have made a greater effort to manufacture the line within its own facilities. However, if it preferred to take a more conservative, wait-and-see approach it would have been justified in seeking a subcontractor.

Before reaching any conclusions, let us evaluate a few more factors. First, a company the size of Lionel benefits greatly through vertical integration of those production processes that it can handle efficiently. To state this more simply, we can say that Lionel would not be effective at refining oil to produce plastics, nor would it be effective at processing wood pulp to manufacture cardboard for its boxes. Yet, Lionel could aggregate a great deal of diverse functions into its corporate functions. Lionel's structure supported a research and development team to engineer products, a tool-making department to produce dies and specialized fixtures, a marketing department to produce catalogues and advertising, as well as

general sales programs, and a variety of production departments, where its products were molded, assembled, painted and lettered. Its vertical integration eliminated the profit margins that subcontractors would require and thus improved Lionel's own pricing and profit requirements.

Why then would Lionel prefer to have Athearn produce H0 trains? There are many possible answers. If Lionel officials believed that the company could not afford the time to design and tool for its own line, then they would have chosen a subcontractor for the purpose of making products in an interim period. The interim would have been that between termination of Rivarossi and establishment of in-house facilities (if Lionel had made the permanent commitment) or between termination of Rivarossi and review of the profitability of H0 (had the commitment been short-term). Additional issues relate to labor costs, overhead costs and capital requirements.

Of these issues, most likely, labor costs and capital requirements are the more significant. In the late 1950s tooling for a single H0 boxcar cost approximately $2,500. Amortizing the costs of the die work for a boxcar over its lengthy useful life (as much as 10-20 years for accounting purposes, longer in actual service for firms such as Athearn), we find a fairly low annual capital expense, which is apportioned over thousands of units of annual output from the die. According to Irvin Athearn, the workers employed in his assembly plants could construct an H0 car from kit components in approximately three to five minutes.[2] Information available from the U.S. Bureau of Census indicates that the average wage for workers in light manufacturing fell between $1.65 and $1.95, thus Athearn's unit cost of assembly then might be estimated between $0.08 and $0.16, somewhat greater than the probable capital cost. Note that additional costs, such as social security and unemployment taxes, are incurred by employers. Relative to the labor, capital and overhead costs, molding and packaging materials contributed only slightly to total cost.

Today, the costs of tooling to produce a locomotive body and mechanism usually amount to ten times the expense of a single piece of rolling stock. Given Athearn's cost of tooling a boxcar at $2500, we might estimate the cost of a locomotive at $25,000. In 1958 Lionel offered a range of H0 models which included Athearn F-7, GP-9 and Husky locomotives, four different passenger cars and six different principal bodies in the freight car line. The capital investment that Lionel would have made had it tooled for its own line in 1958 might be estimated as follows. The larger locomotives have a number of common parts in their mechanisms, thus reducing the marginal cost of adding a second body type to the line. Allowing $25,000 for completion of the first unit, we would add approximately $2,500 for the body of the second unit and another $2,500 for the new chassis. The smaller, simpler Husky locomotive may have

---

1. Interview with Dallas J. Mallerich III, September 8, 1983.

2. Ibid.

required a smaller investment, along the lines of $10,000. Summing these amounts, we calculate $40,000 for the locomotives alone. We have excluded the Pacific and the Docksider which appeared in the 1958 catalogue. The Pacific had not been made at this time, while the Docksider was a carry-over from the Rivarossi agreement.

With passenger cars we find more economies, because trucks, weights and some parts of the dies (roofs and ends between some cars) may be interchangeable. Allowing $2,500 for the first car and $1,500 for each additional type, we calculate the passenger car tooling investment at $7,000. Freight cars, too, use common trucks and weights, however the bodies are more distinctly different. Eight types at $2,500 would cost $20,000. Note that some of the types can be sold in a variety of guises, such as the flatcar, which we find with a boat, an airplane, automobiles, bulkheads or components for a maintenance-of-way caboose. All pieces of rolling stock can be sold also with a variety of paint schemes, thus increasing the utility of the capital investment. The total investment for tooling alone is the sum of locomotive tooling, $30,000, plus passenger tooling, $7,000, and freight car tooling, $20,000, or $57,000. Additional costs would include jigs for painting or lettering the models.

Next on our list is perhaps the greatest concern of assembly plants: labor. Almost concurrent with the introduction of H0, the work force of Lionel made the move toward unionization. While unionization might provide actual improvements in the welfare of individual workers, it tends to discourage the employer from hiring additional employees. As we have seen in this country, a unionized work force also makes the employer more aware of the benefits of mechanization, which quickly becomes a substitute for labor when labor costs increase. Where Athearn employed three hundred workers to produce its entire line, Lionel might have needed seventy-five to manufacture just the H0 line. If we assume that labor is in fact the principal or determinant cost, we must ask, "why did Lionel prefer to pay Athearn for the cost plus a profit margin for the output of seventy-five workers, when Lionel could have added seventy-five workers in its plant?" The most likely answer is the cost differential between unionized and nonunionized labor. Athearn employed the latter, and, in fact, the company split its facilities so that each group of workers would remain in personal contact with management and thereby thwart any incipient tendencies toward unionization.

Now, let us work with several hypotheses to continue our analysis. First, Lionel found that Athearn could produce good-quality models and sell them at a very reasonable price. In preparation of their decision, they invited Athearn to visit New York and to outline a possible contractual relationship. Having made the investment in die work, Athearn could produce additional units from these dies at an extremely low cost. Die work for injection molding wears very slowly, and the cost of plastic for a body shell is minimal. Athearn, then, would bear little or no capital expense in preparing equipment for Lionel; Athearn's principal costs would be labor and overhead. Given the fairly long time spans necessary to prepare die work from original designs and Lionel's introduction of its own models as early as 1960, it might appear that the company's involvement with Athearn arose as a deliberate bridge between termination of the relationship with Rivarossi and the introduction of Lionel H0. However, if one accepts the conclusions regarding Athearn's higher cost efficiency, one must ask why Lionel did not engage a subcontractor throughout

its H0 production. The answer may have more to do with pride than costs. Any Lionel enthusiast feels this pride. The orange and blue package proclaims it; the ubiquitous logo embodies it. Furthermore, Lionel's pride, which arose from domination of the 0 Gauge toy train market, may have suggested that Lionel could achieve the same mass-market success with the hobbyists' H0 train.

We are not certain of the causal relationships. In the case of Athearn, records are not kept longer than necessary for contemporary operation of the business. Irvin Athearn, who made himself available for interview by Dallas Mallerich, has provided only an outline of these events. With a business career of 40 years and a 20-year professional career preceeding that, Irvin Athearn has had a great many business dealings. Since our perspective differs from his, and from those at Lionel, we find that his memories might not include some "pertinent" aspects, and yet he runs a topnotch firm. Executives at Lionel have not achieved quite the tenure of Athearn, and thus we find that primary sources are deceased or retired.

Athearn was an "accepted, good line", stated Lenny Dean, former Lionel service manager. Dean added, "After careful investigation, Lionel went with the people who gave them the best deal — that was Athearn."[3]

In the transitional year of 1958, Lionel offered both the newly-introduced Athearn models and a few Rivarossi carry-overs (excess inventory, probably), including the 0600 tank locomotive and some freight cars. The year brought a banner change in the marketing strategy that would last throughout the production of H0 models. This strategy entailed the duplication of Lionel 0 Gauge models in the smaller scale. According to former Lionel sales manager Sam Belser, "duplicating the 0 line made sense. Lionel 0/027 was a success, so we all thought why couldn't or shouldn't Lionel H0 be?" In his comment, Mr. Belser lends a great deal of support to emphasis on Lionel's pride. He continued to say that, "one of the problems we had with H0 from the very beginning was limitation of our advertising budget. That is why the H0 line was incorporated into the regular 0-027 catalogue in 1958. That was okay, but I always felt there should be a separate catalogue as well. We had to create more enthusiasm and to show that H0 was a vital, viable line on its own. I don't think Lionel ever achieved that important advertising goal."[4]

Lionel's 1958 H0 advance catalogue — quite rare in its own right — gave the retailer some surprises. In many respects it had the effect of "being the first kid on the block" with "never-before-seen" H0 items. Pages two and three of the catalogue state, "Now for the first time! The sales excitement of the new-to-H0 locos, cars, accessories at prices that make H0 scale big sized business. Never before such accuracy, dependability and power in H0 equipment—all backed by the world famous reputation of Lionel!" Nothing was said about the line being produced by Athearn. Lionel certainly produced enthusiastic ad copy; however, the accuracy of those statements leaves something to be desired. Many of Lionel's principal retailers, such as electrical stores and hardware stores, did not purchase or were reluctant to purchase the new H0 line because they did not know much about H0 in general. 1958 became the year of dealer orientation. As the line developed and more

3. Telephone conversation with Lenny Dean, July, 1984; V. Rosa.
4. Telephone interview with Sam Belser, August 14, 1984; V. Rosa.

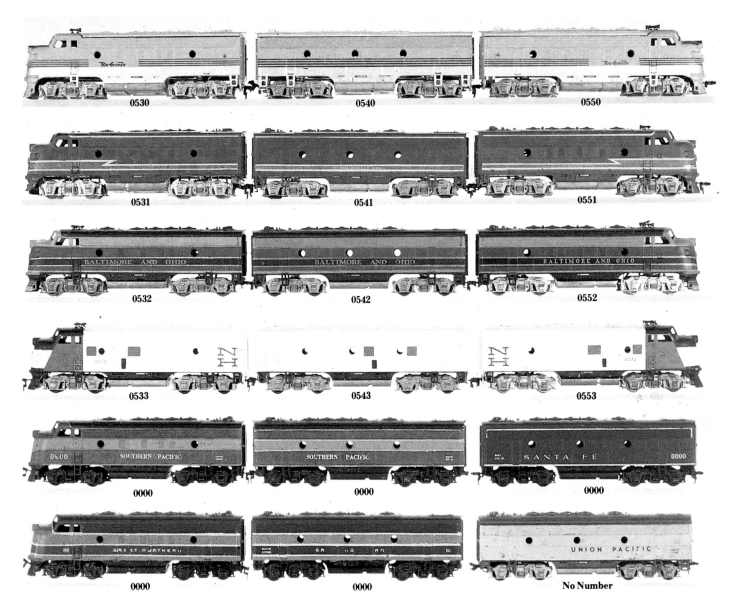

0530	0540	0550
0531	0541	0551
0532	0542	0552
0533	0543	0553
0000	0000	0000
0000	0000	No Number

Six sets of EMD F-7 diesels made by Athearn. Some of these locomotives have road numbers, while others do not. Also, the Lionel logo appears only on some of the models. The models on the top four shelves are production pieces from the Collection of G. Horan. The models on the two bottom shelves are Lionel prototypes. The SP Daylight and the Great Northern Empire Builder paint schemes were used later, when Fundimensions reintroduced the H0 scale Alco. However, none of these four schemes were used in production of the F-7 diesels. Prototypes from the Collection of V. Rosa.

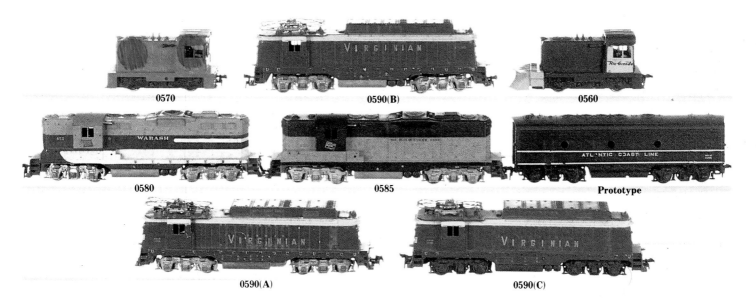

0570   0590(B)   0560

0580   0585   Prototype

0590(A)   0590(C)

Additional Athearn locomotives are shown in this illustration. On the top shelf is an unusual version of the Rectifier locomotive, with the Lionel catalogue number on the long hood, which was sold by Blum's Hobby House. It is flanked by two Husky switchers, the US Navy Husky and the Rio Grande Snowplow. The center shelf shows two GP-9 diesels from regular production and an Atlantic Coast Line prototype. The ACL model was never produced. The bottom shelf shows both of the regular Lionel Virginian Rectifiers, one with silver truck frames and chassis, the other with blackened truck frames and chassis. Neither of the Lionel versions has the Lionel catalogue number on the long hood.

retailers saw the familiar Lionel road names, engines and rolling stock, more retailers did buy H0 trains.

Unfortunately, 1958 was the lowest point of post-World War II train sales. Bernie Paul and Nat Polk have both commented at length at how bad conditions were in the toy and model train industry due to the coincidence of the slotcar road-racing craze and the severe recession. Nat Polk pioneered the model railroad retail industry when, in 1935, he opened a hobby shop in New York City. In addition to providing an accesible outlet for local hobbyists, Polk published an extensive catalogue of hobby merchandise and later extended his business to provide wholesale services to other retailers. Visitors to New York will find Polk's Model Craft Hobbies at 314 5th Avenue, on the lower level. Bernie Paul, founder of A.H.M., has a great deal of experience with importing, wholesaling and retailing model trains. In fact, A.H.M. began to import Rivarossi products shortly after Lionel discontinued its relationship with that firm. Presently, Bernie Paul directs operations of a relatively new company called I.H.M.

"We sold Lionel H0 on its own merit," stated Sam Belser. "It was a competitive line that by 1958 was gradually getting public and retail acceptance. With the right promotion, it could have been one of the greatest lines Lionel ever had."[5] Lionel's name in trains was still magic, so a certain amount of H0 business went to Lionel in 1958. Belser indicated that the marketing strategy for the time being was to get more mass consumer and retailer appeal. By the time the regular consumer catalogue was ready in the fall of 1958, exact-scale references and quality slogans were being dropped and mass appeal concepts were being substituted. Lionel's advanced catalogue states, "For the discriminating hobbyist. This is H0 railroading at its very best." 1958 was the first year in which

one could find a 0197 rotating radar antenna in H0 and a similar 197 in 0 Gauge. Likewise, it was the year of the 0590 Virginian Rectifier with pantograph and headlight—an exact miniature of the new 2329 Virginian Rectifier electric produced in 0 Gauge.

LIONEL/ATHEARN MODELS

As we have suggested, most of the models made for Lionel came directly from the line that Athearn sold under its own name. Usually, Lionel's models differed from standard Athearn products in minor aspects, such as subtle differences in decoration and one or two structural changes. In many cases, only the Lionel logo differentiated one from the other. On the other hand, Lionel did lend some creativity to Athearn's production. The Auto Loader, for instance, duplicated Lionel's 0 Gauge model. To offer this piece, Lionel requested that Athearn produce a two-tier superstructure to place atop his standard flatcar. Subsequently, Athearn produced the Auto Loader, equipped with miniature Cadillacs, for both labels. Lionel also suggested and assisted in creating the 0590 Virginian Rectifier. In fact, this model may be the only joint effort between the two firms. Lionel created the die work for the body shell, which Athearn mounted on its own mechanism. Both firms sold the models, although Athearn soon discontinued its version after the conclusion of its relationship with Lionel.

All of the Athearn cars sold as Lionel products have sprung metal trucks and body-mounted N.M.R.A. couplers. The boxcars have doors that slide inside external guides, while the refrigerator cars have working plug doors and ice hatches. The cabooses are detailed with metal ladders and wire handrails. Athearn may take credit for introducing most of these external details. The trucks and couplers are screw-mounted on all cars. Many Lionel/Athearn items fall into the "scarce" or "rare" categories of Lionel H0 models, and although one might expect to pay dearly for a particular item, it may still elude the collector.

5. Ibid.

This is the standard Athearn version of the Virginian rectifier, which, unlike the Lionel version, has "0590" on its hood. The Athearn version does not have "Blt. by Lionel" on it. T. Shepler Collection.

Athearn's 1958 H0 line provided many of the familiar Lionel road names and paint schemes. F-7 diesels in separate A-B-A combinations were available in road names that included Denver and Rio Grande 0530, Milwaukee Road 0531, Baltimore and Ohio 0532 and New Haven 0533. Also new were the Virginian Rectifier 0590 and the GP-9 in Milwaukee Road 0585 and Wabash 0580 liveries. Later, the rectifier was decorated by Lionel for Pennsylvania (1960) and New Haven (1959-1960) liveries.[6] The 1958 consumer catalogue states that the Virginian rectifier is a model of GE's type El-C 3300 electric locomotive. This is one piece that was produced under both corporate names, Lionel and Athearn. The Athearn 1958-1959 catalogue flyer clearly shows the Virginian rectifier and states, "New, the Virginian Rectifier, a kit with power, is $7.95." It has an 0590 number on the cab. Close scrutiny of the picture in the Athearn catalogue reveals a remote "Blt. by Lionel" on the cab. If Athearn made the piece, then why did they use Lionel's photo? Our research has shown that Athearn did not make the cab for the Virginian rectifier — Lionel did. The Lionel part number 0590-5 is on the inside of the cabs of both the Athearn and Lionel/Athearn pieces. In 1958 Athearn made the motor mechanism and frame. The version sold under the Athearn label came with silver trucks and frame, no herald decal, no lights and no reflective material inside the body. Athearn's model featured wire handrails, whereas Lionel had none. The Athearn version, which carried the number "0590" at the end of the long hood, was not heavily advertised; it disappeared from the market in late 1958 or early 1959.

The Lionel/Athearn version (the model sold under the Lionel label) differs somewhat from the Athearn version. It has chemically blackened trucks and frames in some cases, though it may be found with the silver trucks and frames. (Trucks and frames are interchangeable between these models.) The road name on Lionel's model appears lower on the side and in lighter yellow print than on the Athearn version. A herald decal appears on the front, and "0590" appears on the long hood. The Lionel version also has a headlight and reflective material in the headlight area. A black horn appears above the cab headlight. "Blt. by Lionel" is rubber-stamped on each side of the short hood; however, there is no Lionel logo per se. Both versions feature the Athearn Hi-F rubber band drive. Later, Lionel introduced its own mechanism for the New Haven (1959-1960) and Pennsylvania (1960) rectifiers. Since 1958, Athearn has not produced any rectifier locomotives, which probably indicates that Athearn does not have the dies. Whether or not the tooling has been preserved remains unknown.

The 1958 rectifiers, GP-9s and Husky switchers, 0560 D&RG and 0570 Navy Yard were all belt-driven locomotives. Although Lionel promoted the idea that belt driven locomotives were super quiet, the company did not convince consumers that belts were better than gears. The "neoprene belts" were 0 ring transmissions positioned between the motor shaft and the drive axles. They were not consistent with the quality that Lionel usually produced, and they caused headaches for service stations. The rubber belts, Lenny Dean explained, "went bad and expanded as we tried to store them in our warehouses". They were a "severe service manager's nightmare, not knowing whether the shipment of neoprene drive bands to a service station was a fresh or shopworn, dryrotted batch of rubber belts."[7]

The Athearn line continued with a little Navy switcher 0570 (black shell painted blue; Hi-F drive) and a Denver & Rio Grande 0560 snowplow. The Lionel logo (L within a circle) and a variation in cab sides distinguish the Lionel/Athearn piece, which has black and yellow cab sides, from the regular Athearn model, which has orange cab sides. In 1958 both yard switchers had Athearn rubber band drives. By 1959 Lionel had begun to produce its own mechanisms, although Athearn still supplied some of the body shells. Later, Lionel made its own copy of the body shell.

The Boston & Maine 0615LT (4-6-2) Pacific with full Walschaerts valve gear, which Lionel catalogued in 1958, has eluded H0 collectors for good reason: it was never made. Athearn designed this piece, with a Hi-F rubber band drive, for its own line, but preproduction showed the drive to be terribly inappropriate for a steam locomotive. Athearn also found that the plastic drive wheels originally designed for the locomotive would collect metal from the rails and become too slick for sufficient traction. Unsatisfied with the samples, Athearn removed the locomotive from the production schedule. The company later designed a gear-driven mechanism for this locomotive, but Lionel had begun its own production by that time. There is no evidence that preproduction samples were made for Lionel. It is interesting to note that the engine depicted in Lionel's 1958 catalogue with "full Walschaerts valve gear" is actually a Fleishmann H0 Pacific made in Germany.

The 5714 New Haven passenger set released in 1958 has different numbers on the boxes and cars, similar to some of American Flyer's practices. In other words, the number on the car is different from the catalogue or order number that appears on the box end and in the catalogue. Athearn usually decorated rolling stock with prototypical numbers, while Lionel used their catalogue number, which was part of a series for order and inventory control. This inconsistency was resolved after Lionel began to produce its own line in 1959. The New Haven F-7s had a Lionel catalogue number of 0533-1. The Athearn number on the side was 0272. An orange Lionel "L" also appeared on the sides. The set also came with a Lionel number 0700-1 baggage which was numbered 3406 in black on the side. A Lionel 0701-1 Pullman actually numbered 3150, an 0702-1 Vista Dome numbered 500 on the side and a 0703-1 observation car numbered 3246. There are many inconsistencies with Lionel/Athearn lettering. Some mint pieces have shown up in Lionel boxes without the logos. But, a word of

---

6. McComas & Tuohy, p. 105.

7. Lenny Dean, ibid.

0872-1   0866-25   0836(A)

0864-25   0864-200(A)   0864-150(A)

0864-50(B)   0864-50(A)   0864-225

0872-50(C)   0872-50(A)   0872-50(A)

0864-250(B)   0815   0864-175

0801   0877   0860

The freight cars that Athearn made for Lionel carry a variety of interesting paint schemes, as well as numerous variations in the lettering and application of Lionel logos. The State of Maine cars on the third shelf from the top display the large (left) and small (right) logos. The three Santa Fe cars on the fourth shelf represent only two variations of the three variations.

The "Super Chief" variation shown at left is the rarest. It has the "SHIP AND TRAVEL" slogan on the opposite side; however, it carries the number "8293". The second and third car on this shelf are both the first variation, which has the number "8392" on both sides and the two different sides lettered as shown.

caution to the novice, if a piece of Athearn equipment is not in its original box, it should be accepted as Lionel only if it has the Lionel logo on it.

New rolling stock made by Athearn in 1958 included a 0800 Flatcar with airplane, 0801 Flatcar with boat, 0879 Wrecker Crane, 0815 Gulf Chemical car, 0860 Derrick car, 0814 Auto Loader (which Lionel requested from Athearn), 0824 Flatcar with two automobiles, 0817 Milwaukee caboose, 0865 Gondola with cannisters, 0819-100 Boston & Maine work caboose which also came in many other road names, 0866-25 Santa Fe cattle car, 0836 Lehigh Valley hopper, 0877 Miscellaneous car and 0872-1 Fruit Growers Express. The 0864 Lionel H0 boxcar series was introduced with all the 0 Gauge 6464 series road names such as State of Maine, Monon, Minneapolis & St. Louis, Timken, Rutland, etc., and a line of New Haven passenger cars (0700-0703). Track for 1958 train sets was produced by Atlas Tool & Die Co., while all of the accessories were produced by Lionel.

A LITTLE CONFUSION

Athearn's production of H0 for Lionel continued into 1959-1960, although Athearn no longer served as principal supplier of the line. In these years, Lionel/Athearn products were in almost every case the same as kits sold in the Athearn line, although Lionel sold these models only in ready-to-run form. Until the mid-1960s Athearn's advertisements clearly show the Lionel logo on some of its cars. This probably occurred for two reasons. First, Athearn accidentally photographed models with Lionel logos. Second, Athearn recycled advertisements as much as possible. Thus Athearn continued to illustrate Lionel/Athearn models although it no longer produced them.

Some confusion arises from Lionel's 1958 catalogue, because both Athearn and Rivarossi models are illustrated. The black New Haven boxcar, carried forward from the Lionel/Rivarossi line of 1957, appears in the catalogue. The Lionel/Athearn New Haven boxcar, not illustrated, is orange. In the 1959 catalogue two Athearn boxcars, Timken and State of Maine, appear alongside the Lionel boxcars introduced that year. Athearn provided caboose shells into the 1960s, but, with the exception of these, the two boxcars and a few passenger cars, the Athearn items had disappeared from the catalogue by 1961.

Lionel's logo does appear, in either of two sizes, on most of the Athearn items made from 1958 to 1960, although there are some cars that do not have a logo. The latter typically appear in 1958 train sets. The first runs of Lionel/Athearn had such a small logo that it hardly could be seen. It measured only 1/16" in diameter. On later cars, a larger, 1/8" logo appears. The position of the logo varies somewhat. Lionel cars have other features not found on the cars sold under the Athearn label. Both Lionel and Athearn reefers have operating doors and ice hatches (contemporary Athearn reefers do not have operating doors). The boxcars all have an early door that rides inside door guides. The claw foot-type doors appear only on one Lionel car, the 0866-25 Santa Fe stock car. The simple sliding door used on Lionel cars operates more freely than the claw foot door, but the latter is still used on current Athearn models. The brakewheels, roofwalk and door guides are press-fit into holes in the body and sometimes painted to match the body color. Steps, grab-irons and ladders are details in the body casting.

The Athearn cars have good rivet detail, and they are weighted with a metal strip held between the floor and the undercarriage of the car. The 1958 catalogue clearly shows Lionel numbers on the Athearn cars, but only a few passenger cars were made that way. All other items carried only Athearn numbers on the items and Lionel numbers on the cartons. The cars listed after this paragraph can be found in early 1958 Lionel sets without the logo on them.

Brown L.V. Hopper	Blue Wabash Boxcar
Red U.P. Crane	Tuscan Michigan Central Gondola
Orange Gulf Tank	Tuscan Reading Flatcar with Stakes
Yellow F.G.E. Reefer	Black Erie Flatcar with
Orange El Capitan Reefer	two Automobiles

LIONEL/ATHEARN MECHANISMS

Hi-F rubber band drive of Athearn F-7 locomotives.

All of the Athearn locomotives sold by Lionel in 1958-1959 were powered with the Hi-F rubber band drive, which Athearn had introduced in 1956. This includes the F-7 units in four road names, one rectifier, two hustlers, one snowplow and two geeps marketed in Lionel packaging. The frame of the F-7 is a one-piece metal casting; the trucks are also cast in metal with drum-type axles approximately 3/8" in diameter. The five-pole, double-shaft motor is fastened to the center of the frame with a single screw. The frame also has two vertical lugs cast into it, both above and below the floor of the frame. The bottom portion of the lug passes through the truck frame and acts as a pivot for the trucks. On dummy A and B units the trucks are secured to these lugs with a small rubber washer that slips over the tip of the lug. The top portion of the lug has a small drilled hole in it and acts as a guide for the motor shaft extension. This extension is a length of steel rod held to the motor shaft with a rubber coupling. The wire extensions and lugs are found on all Lionel band driven units built by Athearn, with the exception of the Hustler locomotive. Four black neoprene rubber bands couple the shaft and the four drum-type axles to drive all eight wheels on all power units. The models have electrical pickup in both trucks; they have metal wheel sets and plastic axles. All powered units are lighted with a bulb that is retained by a metal clip fastened to the front of the frame with a single screw. The frame also has cast-on coupler pads at each end below the floor line and tabs at either side. The tabs hold the shell to the frame while the coupler pads accept both the coupler and coupler housing, again fastened with one screw. Except those used to mount the couplers, there are no screws in dummy A or B units. Dummy models have metal axles and plastic wheels. To service the A units, the front coupler must be removed through the opening in the front of the shell. On powered units, the trucks must be disassembled in order to replace the rubber bands. This is accomplished by removing two small screws at the top of the truck frame, slipping the top of the band over the drum axle and reassembling the truck. It was a tedious job for a new modeler. The very early Athearn frames carry the Athearn name cast onto the bottom, but they were never used on units sold as Lionel. Lionel units came with both silver and blackened trucks and frames.

THE RECTIFIER & GP-9 MECHANISM

Hi-F rubber band drive used in both Rectifier and GP-9 locomotives.

The same frame appears on both the electric and GP-9. It is square at both ends, and it has a half-inch extension to support the platform and steps at each end of the locomotive shell and to hold the coupler pad. The headlight fixture is fastened under the front of the frame with the same screw that holds the front coupler. The two round tabs on each side of the frame secure the shell. The coupler pockets and covers on these frames are cast metal. Just to the rear of the fuel tanks, there are two black plastic air tanks pressed into a hole in the top of the frame. The motor and drive shaft are the same as those used on F-units. The frame and trucks are unpainted silvery metal.

HUSTLER MECHANISMS

Hi-F rubber band drive of Athearn Husky switchers.

The Hustler frame and motor designs follow the basic pattern of the other mechanism. The frame is cast metal, and there is a five-pole double-shaft motor. Drum-type axles and metal wheel sets are driven by rubber bands mounted on the drive shafts. No wire extensions appear. The model is equipped with the same type of light fixture as found on the F-7; it is located in the cab of the locomotive. The couplers are slightly different, in that they are mounted in notches in the frame; however, they do have a metal cover, which is attached with a screw. To replace the rubber band, one has to remove the two screws

from the right side of the frame, but first the body shell must be removed to reveal these concealed screws. The mechanism for the Rio Grande Snowplow is blackened, but otherwise similar.

LIONEL/ATHEARN LOCOMOTIVES

Having described mechanisms in the foregoing segments, we have limited descriptions of individual units to that of the body shell, trim, paint scheme and lettering.

                                              Gd Exc Mt

EMD F-7 DIESELS

NOTE: These locomotives are grouped in A-B-A sets for each road name.

0530 DENVER & RIO GRANDE Powered A unit; roof painted silver, from above the cab windows back to the end of the roof, and matching lower side panels, air tank covers and ladders; pale, flat orangish-yellow cab roof, end, headlight area and top two sets of side panels; single black pin stripe between orange and silver at roof line; four black pin stripes on the side panels; black nose top; lower side striping broken approximately 1-1/2" above the air tanks, where the road name appears in black; road name appears a second time in black on a decal located just above the pilot; two clear plastic headlight lenses; two black plastic horns, number boards and steps; available for separate sale in A-B-A combinations or in set 5715, with an A-A combination; Lionel catalogue numbers appear only on the carton; catalogued in 1958 only.
(A) Lionel logo 1/16", on lower side panel just above last cab ladder.

                                              25   45   80

(B) Lionel logo appears above the black striping in the last orangish side panel; logo is larger and more easily seen; uncatalogued; 1959.

                                              25   45   80

0540 DENVER & RIO GRANDE Dummy B unit; fully painted silver roof and matching lower side panels; black striping as described for A unit; eight cast-on steps; no lettering or numbers.
(A) Lionel logo 1/16", on lower side panel just above last cab ladder.

                                              30   40   60

(B) Lionel logo appears above the black striping in the last orangish side panel; logo is larger and more easily seen; uncatalogued; 1959.

                                              30   40   60

0550 DENVER & RIO GRANDE Dummy A unit; matches powered A unit, as described.   **30   40   60**

0531 MILWAUKEE ROAD Powered A unit; painted dark semi-gloss gray; yellow pin stripe across cab roof continues down the sides to the end of the unit at the roof line; bright flat orange nose, enclosing both headlights but not the number boards; nose coloration outlined with yellow pin stripe above and below the orange patch; "2376" in yellow on the side, below the cab window; road name appears between the two portholes on the side stripe; 1/16" diameter Lionel logo in the last orange side panel, just behind the rear cab door; road name appears a second time on a silver and black decal just above the pilot; two decorative horns and headlight lenses; no Lionel numbers appear on the unit; catalogued in 1958 only.   **35   45   80**

0541 MILWAUKEE ROAD Dummy B unit; painted to match the powered with corresponding striping; road name appears in the last orange stripe; no numbers; Lionel logo located as described for A unit.   **30   40   60**

0551 MILWAUKEE ROAD Dummy A unit; matches powered A unit, as described.   **30   40   60**

0532 BALTIMORE & OHIO Powered A unit; flat black; painted roof; gray nose and windshield extending past the cab windows to the end of the body; royal blue nose and side panels; herald appears on decal located under the lower headlight on a black stripe that runs back to the rear of the unit and separates the blue panel; all colors separated by gold pin stripes; cast-on number boards; two headlights and decorative horns; 1/16" diameter Lionel logo located on the black stripe between the cab door and end of the body; these are the most common of the F units; catalogue

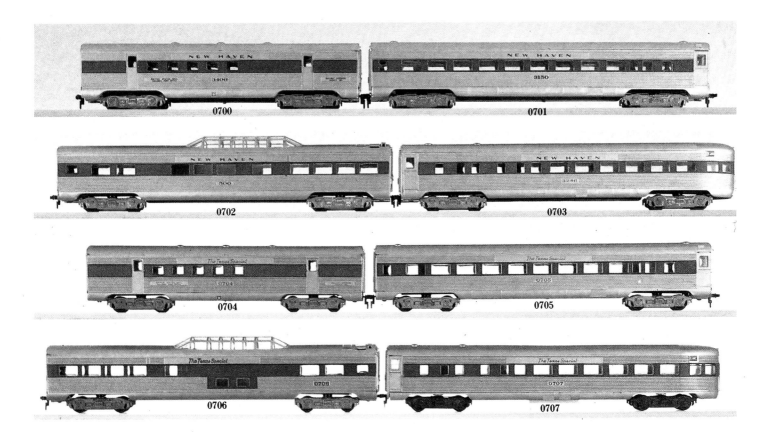

0700　0701　0702　0703　0704　0705　0706　0707

Shown are the early type Athearn cars without the battery box area between the trucks. The New Haven cars, which were catalogued only in 1958, are found only with this body type.

number appears on carton, but not on unit. The gray and blue used on units sold by Athearn of the same period are much darker in shading.

30　45　60

0542　BALTIMORE & OHIO Dummy B unit; flat black roof and ends; sides match those on powered A unit; 1/16" diameter gold Lionel logo located above ladder in last side panel; road name in gold lettering on black stripe. **25　28　30**

0552　BALTIMORE & OHIO Dummy A unit; matches description of powered A unit; catalogued in 1958 only for separate sale in A-B-A combination and in set 5713, with A-B diesels. **25　28　30**

0533　NEW HAVEN Powered A unit; flat white, painted body, including roof and side panels from just behind the cab windows to the rear of unit; flat black cab roof, pilot, ladders, windshield area, nose and air tanks; flat orange cab sides; one small black square and two orange squares appear on white side panel; orange "N" and "H" appear in the last two white side panels; no road name; "0272" directly under first porthole and Lionel logo under the rear porthole, both in the white portion of the lower side panel; catalogued in 1958 only, for separate sale, and in passenger set 5714 with A-A diesels. A similar model was sold in the Penn Line H0 range of the period; in fact, the model featured the same paint scheme and road number. Of course, the Penn Line unit has no Lionel logo, and the paint is glossy rather than flat. Still, the Penn Line model could be mistaken for Lionel at first inspection. **35　50　60**

0543　NEW HAVEN Dummy B unit; entire body painted white; flat black air tanks, ladders and floor sill; orange "NH"; no full road name; no road number; 1/16" diameter Lionel logo between rear door and end of unit; two small orange squares and one black square on side. **30　35　40**

0553　NEW HAVEN Dummy A unit; matches description of powered A unit. **30　35　40**

0560　DENVER RIO GRANDE "SNOWPLOW" Powered; flat black, painted body; light, semi-gloss yellow cab sides; road name and 1/16" Lionel logo appear in black on cab side; Lionel logo directly under "R" in "Rio Grande"; black decorative horn on each side of hood; darker, yellowish-orange non-operating snowplow blade snaps onto the front of

body; cast-on headlight housing at each end, but only cab end lighted; no headlight lenses; no road number; catalogued in 1958-59 as a separate item; Lionel number appears on carton only; snowplow often missing. Athearn sold the same unit in the same period with orange cab sides and a yellow plow blade. Very rare. **55　75　150**

0570　NAVY YARD SWITCHER Powered; same body as 0560 snowplow; painted light blue; two black plastic horns and headlights; the headlight housing on the Athearn units is very small, while the later Lionel locomotive has a much larger light casting; white, stamped lettering on cab sides; "NAVY YARD NEW YORK" and "51"; 1/16" Lionel logo directly under "N" in "NAVY"; "HUSTLER" runs vertically on the front radiator and is part of casting; Lionel numbers on carton only; catalogued in 1958 only, as a separate item and with set 5705; it was not reintroduced in 1959 when Lionel made their own switchers; difficult to find and considered rare.

50　75　150

0580　WABASH GP-9 Powered; tri-color body; light gray cab and upper portion of body; dark blue lower portion trimmed in white; four blue fans on roof; road name, in white lettering, on blue portion of long hood; 1/8" diameter Lionel logo appears just before the road name; "452" on blue portion of short hood; four headlight inserts; no handrails; blue Wabash flag on gray portion of cab; two brass decorative horns; separate cab casting snaps onto body shell; Lionel numbers appear on carton only; catalogued in 1958 as a separate item and in set 5707; very rare. The Athearn Wabash unit of the period had a blue cab with a white flag and no Lionel logo; note that these cabs are interchangeable. **45　75　160**

0585　MILWAUKEE ROAD GP-9 Powered; flat black cab, upper portion of body, pilots and floor sill; bright flat orange roof fans and lower portion of body; only the road name appears on long hood; white logo on cab side; no other markings or numbers, except Lionel logo on the orange side panel just past the rear cab door; wire handrails and decorative horn present; Lionel number on carton; catalogued in 1958 only as a separate item; rare.

45　75　160

0590　VIRGINIAN RECTIFIER Powered; painted light blue; yellow, 1/4" wide band around the entire locomotive at roof line; "Built by Lionel"

0830(A)   0879(B)

0865(A)   0865(B)

0814(A)   0814(B)

These Athearn items fit well with Lionel's interest in presenting "play value" in train sets. The piggyback flatcar has the small logo, as does the Union Pacific crane. The boom of the crane may be operated with the small metal crank that Lionel sold with the model. The Michigan Central gondolas were produced in 1958 (left) and 1959 (right); the latter car came with six rather than five cannisters as found on the former. The Auto Loaders changed in these years also, with the car being lettered for Reading in 1958.

stamped in yellow on the short hood just in front of the cab door; road name spelled out and centered on the long hood; brass pantograph mounted on roof with four metal pins; light insert at each end, but only cab end lighted; Virginian logo decal on the front of shell. The Virginian disappeared in 1959. It was replaced with Lionel's 0591 New Haven Rectifier using the same shell, which has the part number cast into the inside roof; this part number appears in all rectifiers whether sold by Lionel or Athearn. It was always assumed that the Virginian was an Athearn locomotive, because of the rubber band drive used to power it. However, the model is actually a combined effort: Lionel manufactured the body shells, while Athearn decorated the body shells and manufactured the mechanism.

(A) No number on end of long hood; silver frame and trucks.   55   80   200
(B) Lionel number on end of long hood; darker blue body; sold by Blum's Hobby House in the early 1960s in Athearn sets; as far as can be determined, this locomotive was never sold by Lionel; V. Rosa Collection.
                                                          NRS

(C) Similar to (A), but black frame and trucks.   55   80   200

PASSENGER CARS

Between 1958 and 1962 Lionel catalogued a variety of road names for their four types of streamlined passenger cars. The four car types had been made by Athearn as far back as 1956. All have plastic bodies, clear plastic window inserts and metal four-wheel trucks with N.M.R.A.-type couplers. Each truck is secured to the floor with one screw. During the period in which the Lionel/Athearn cars were catalogued, they were constructed in two ways. Each is considered rare.

Type I Body: In 1958, the first cars have a one-piece body with a separate flat floor casting which snaps into the walls of the body. The only details on the outer floor are the coupler pockets and floor bracings. These early cars are found with

part of the main bracing and coupler pocket removed (to accept the talgo-type truck used by Lionel). The trucks are silver. New Haven cars are found only with this type of construction.

Type II Body: The second type of construction appeared in 1961. It was catalogued in the Pennsylvania set 5756. The main changes occurred in the floor design, which was revised to have a cast battery box in the center of the floor. The coupler pockets are absent, and the skirting of the car body is part of the floor, rather than the car side. A half-inch high wall was added inside to hold the car together. The trucks are black, and they have a pivot pin cast into them. The pin passes through the floor of the car, and it is fastened from inside with a single screw.

The Texas Special and Pennsylvania cars have both types of bodies. Early cars are more difficult to find than later cars, because they were produced for a shorter time.

NEW HAVEN PASSENGER CARS Painted silver; dull orange band through window area; black lettering; "NEW HAVEN" appears centered above windows; no Lionel numbers appear on cars; no Lionel logo; catalogue number appears on carton; catalogued in 1958 only, and never reintroduced in the Lionel line; catalogued in set 5714 and as separate items; prized when found in their original boxes; rare.

0700	**Baggage**	"3406" on car side.	20	45	55
0701	**Pullman**	"3150" on car side.	20	45	55
0702	**Vista Dome**	"500" on car side.	20	45	55
0703	**Observation**	"3246" on car side.	20	45	55

TEXAS SPECIAL PASSENGER CARS Painted silver; dark red striping in window area; red lettering; road name centered above windows; catalogued first in 1959 as separate items and in set 5732. The cars were headed by Lionel's new Alco units; two powered 0566 and a dummy B 0576 pulled the four cars. In 1960 the cars were catalogued in set 5770; this set

Underside of an Athearn boxcar. Note body-mounted couplers and sheet metal weight, which is held in place by plastic ribs.

consisted of the same A-B-A diesels, but the consist included two 0706 Vista Dome cars, one 0705 Pullman, plus one 0707 Observation. The cars were not shown in the 1961 catalogue, but they reappeared in 1962 in set 14054, which featured a powered 0566 and the same consist found in set 5770; the cars were never shown again after 1961.

0704	Baggage	20	45	55
0705	Pullman	20	45	55
0706	Vista Dome	20	45	55
0707	Observation	20	45	55

PENNSYLVANIA PASSENGER CARS Deep tuscan, painted body; black roof; yellow-gold lettering; road name centered above windows; Lionel catalogue number appears on number board below windows; first catalogued in 1960 in set 5742 with the Pennsylvania Rectifier and three cars, the Baggage, Vista Dome and Observation. In 1961 set 5756 featured the same consist and a 0635 Pacific. The 0711 Pullman was catalogued in 1960 as a separate item, and it is the most difficult passenger car to find of all the Athearn for Lionel cars. Discontinued in 1961, these are very attractive cars.

0708	Baggage	20	45	55
0709	Vista Dome	20	45	55
0710	Observation	20	45	55
0711	Pullman	60	75	150

FREIGHT CARS

In almost every case, Lionel/Athearn rolling stock is identical to the items sold under the Athearn label at the time. Only the Lionel logo on the car or a Lionel package distinguishes the items from regular Athearn production. Except those found in the early-1958 Lionel sets, all of the Athearn cars have sprung metal trucks and body-mounted N.M.R.A. couplers.

BOXCARS

0864-25 NEW YORK CENTRAL Red and gray, painted body with matching door and door guides; unpainted black roofwalk and brakewheel; white lettering; numbered "174477"; 1/8" diameter Lionel logo appears in the gray portion of the first panel to the right of the door; Lionel numbers appear only on the carton; catalogued in 1958 only; very rare.

	20	45	80

0864-50 STATE OF MAINE Red, white and blue, painted body, with matching door; four-letterboard door; three boards carry the lettering "OF" and the letters "D" and "U" from "PRODUCTS"; white stripe on door seldom matches white of car side; black and white lettering; numbered "5206"; Lionel logo appears in the last panel to the left of the door; catalogued in 1958; Lionel's own version replaced it in 1959.
(A) 1/16" diameter Lionel logo; "AND" on door.   20   45   80
(B) 1/8" diameter Lionel logo; no "AND" on door.   20   45   80

0864-150 MINNEAPOLIS & ST. LOUIS Dull orange, painted body; white lettering; numbered "52673"; Lionel logo appears just above the door guide in the second panel to the right of the door; unpainted black door guides, roofwalk and brakewheel; four-letterboard door as found on the State of Maine car; Lionel number appears only on carton; catalogued in 1958 only; very difficult to find.
(A) 1/16" diameter Lionel logo; unpainted door.   25   45   80
(B) 1/8" diameter Lionel logo; painted door.   25   45   80

0864-175 TIMKEN Bright yellow, painted body; 1/2" white band on side; matching door and door guides; unpainted black brakewheel and roofwalk; brown "TIMKEN", "ROLLER FREIGHT" and "88" on the white band at the upper left of the door; 1/16" diameter brown Lionel logo appears just below the road number; red "ROLLER FREIGHT" logo at the right of the door; catalogued in 1958 and 1959; no Lionel number on car; discontinued in 1960; extremely hard to find.   25   55   120

0864-200 MONON Brown, painted body; white lettering; numbered "3029"; 1/16" diameter Lionel logo appears in the fifth panel to the left of the door, just below the grab-iron; Lionel number appears only on carton; catalogued in 1958 only. The catalogue illustration depicts a black car with "The Hoosier Line" appearing in black letters on a white stripe at the top of the car; however, the car was not made this way. Very rare.
(A) Brown door, roofwalk and door guides, painted to match car sides.
  20   30   60
(B) Unpainted black roofwalk and brakewheel.   20   30   60

0864-225 CENTRAL OF GEORGIA Tuscan, painted body; silver side panels and door; silver and tuscan lettering; red "CENTRAL OF GEORGIA" on a yellow square; unpainted black brakewheel and roofwalk; numbered "7402"; 1/16" diameter Lionel logo appears in the last side panel to the left of the door; catalogued in 1958; discontinued in 1959.
  20   30   40

0864-250 WABASH Light blue, painted body, with matching door and door guides; unpainted black brakewheel and roofwalk; white lettering; red Wabash flag appears in a white heart-shaped background at the right of the door; numbered "6287"; Lionel number appears only on carton; catalogued in 1958 only; discontinued in 1959. Unlike the 0 Gauge counterpart, this car does not operate.
(A) Without Lionel logo; found in early 1958 sets.   20   30   40
(B) 1/16" diameter Lionel logo appears in the second panel to the right of the door.   20   30   40

REFRIGERATOR CARS

0872-1 FRUIT GROWERS EXPRESS REFRIGERATOR Dull yellow, painted sides; tuscan roof and ends; unpainted roofwalk and brakewheel; black lettering; numbered "9253"; Lionel logo appears in the fifth panel to the left of the doors; operating doors and ice hatches; cast-on ladders and six steps; catalogue number appears on carton only; catalogued only in 1958; replaced in 1959 by Lionel's Railway Express Refrigerator.   25   50   85

0872-50 SANTA FE REFRIGERATOR Dull orange, painted sides roof and ends; black and white Santa Fe cross herald; black lettering; operating doors and ice hatches; catalogue number appears on carton only; catalogued in 1958; difficult to find with the door unbroken. Dallas Mallerich suggests that the variations found probably arose because of batches being mixed between the stages of this printing job which had different lettering each side. The same road numbers, and a variety of slogans, are found on variations in regular Athearn production.

(A) "El Capitan" slogan on one side, "Ship and Travel" on other; numbered "8392" on both sides; Lionel logo appears at the left of the door below the grab-iron.   **15 20 50**

(B) Similar to (A); numbered "8293" on both sides; Lionel logo appears only on the "El Capitan" side.   **15 20 50**

(C) "Route of the Super Chief" on one side, "Ship and Travel" on the other; "8293" on both sides; 1/16" diameter Lionel logo; see photograph; extremely rare.   **NRS**

STOCK CARS

0866-25 STOCK CAR Light green, painted body, door and door guides; claw foot door; door guides cast into car side; two letterboards cast onto the left-hand side of the car; yellow lettering; "SANTA FE" appears on upper board; "50656" appears on lower board; 1/16" diameter Lionel logo appears in the third panel to the left of the door; unpainted black brakewheel and roofwalk; catalogue number appears on carton only; catalogued in 1958 only; available uncatalogued in 1959; discontinued in 1959; replaced by Lionel's Poultry Car; fairly common. This is the only Athearn stock car sold by Lionel.   **10 15 40**

GONDOLAS

0865 GONDOLA White lettering; "MICHIGAN CENTRAL R.R."; numbered "350623"; 1/8" Lionel logo appears at the floor line in the fifth side panel; loaded with six red unmarked cannisters; catalogued in 1958.

(A) Tuscan body; 1/16" diameter Lionel logo; 1958 only.   **8 10 20**

(B) Black body; 1/8" diameter logo; uncatalogued; 1959.   **8 10 20**

TANK CARS

0815 GULF TANK CAR Unpainted black frame, platform and lower half of tank body; bright orange, painted top half of body, dome and ends; black band runs vertically under the platform down to the frame; lettered "Gulf Oil Corporation"; numbered "2605"; no Lionel logo; wire handrails on platform; stamped metal ladders from platform downward to the frame; brakewheel; catalogued in 1958-59 as a separate item and in sets; Lionel number appears on carton only; discontinued in 1960. This is the first HO tank car sold by Lionel; none were sold in 1957.   **10 15 45**

FLATCARS and MISCELLANEOUS CARS

0800 FLATCAR WITH AIRPLANE 40' flatcar painted black; white lettering; "Nickel Plate Railroad"; numbered "1958", the year the car was introduced; 1/16" diameter Lionel logo appears in the second side panel; plastic single-engine Beechcraft airplane with landing gear and prop; separate wings carried alongside airplane body; black plastic mounting carriage snapped onto floor of car; load often broken in some way; catalogued in 1958-59.

(A) Airplane with unpainted black underbody; dull orange, painted top portion, tail and wings.   **15 20 45**

(B) Airplane with unpainted black underbody; silver, painted top portion, tail and wings.   **15 20 45**

0801 FLATCAR WITH BOAT 40' flatcar; dark brown, painted body; blue and white plastic boat, same as that used on the 0 Gauge counterpart; white lettering; "SEABOARD"; numbered "42806"; black plastic brakewheel; Lionel logo appears near end of car; two black plastic carriages snap onto car floor and retain load; Lionel number appears only on carton; catalogued in 1958-59; replaced in 1960 by 0801-200. Reportedly, this car has been seen

with a different road number; verification of other road number(s) requested.   **15 20 45**

0811-25 FLATCAR WITH STAKES White lettering; "READING"; numbered "9440"; black plastic brakewheel; 1/16" diameter Lionel logo appears just before the road name; one dozen steel stakes; Lionel number appears on carton only; very difficult to find.

(A) Painted brown; 1958.   **10 15 40**

(B) Painted black; 1959.   **10 15 40**

0814 50' AUTO-LOADER Tuscan, painted flatcar; black automobile rack superstructure; loaded with two white station wagons and two red sedans; white lettering; automobile rack lettered "EVANS AUTO-LOADER"; Lionel logo appears in the second side panel; catalogue number appears on carton only; catalogued in 1958-59; illustration does not show station wagons as part of the load.

(A) Flatcar lettered "READING"; numbered "40125"; 1/16" diameter Lionel logo; 1958.   **15 20 45**

(B) Flatcar lettered "NEW YORK CENTRAL"; numbered "499300"; 1/8" diameter Lionel logo; 1959.   **15 20 45**

0824 AUTO FLAT Flatcar with two automobiles; white lettering; "ERIE"; numbered "74286"; 1/16" diameter Lionel logo appears in the side panel just before the road name; Lionel number appears on the carton only; catalogued in 1958-59; replaced in 1960 by Lionel's 0824-200.

(A) Black car, as shown in catalogue illustration for separate item and set 5713; small Lionel logo.   **10 20 35**

(B) Red car, as shown in catalogue illustration for set 5709.   **10 20 35**

0830 PIGGYBACK FLATCAR Same body as used for the 1958 Auto Loader; tuscan; white lettering; "READING"; numbered "40125"; Lionel logo appears in the second side panel; two white plastic trailers; "Cooper-Jarret Trucking Co." on orange arrow on trailer side; black plastic trailer rack snaps onto car floor; catalogue number appears on carton only; catalogued in 1958-59.

(A) 1/16" Lionel logo; 1958.   **10 20 45**

(B) 1/8" Lionel logo; 1959; more difficult to find.   **10 20 45**

0877 MISCELLANEOUS CAR 40' bulkhead flatcar; painted flat black; white lettering; "ILLINOIS CENTRAL"; numbered "63210"; 1/16" diameter Lionel logo; one brakewheel; no load came with car; catalogue number appears on carton only; catalogued in 1958 only; available uncatalogued in 1959; discontinued 1960; much scarcer than the similar Rivarossi car.   **10 15 40**

HOPPER CARS

0836 LEHIGH VALLEY HOPPER 40' car; brown, painted body; white lettering; "LEHIGH VALLEY" spelled across side; "L.V." and "4127" in first large side panel; diamond-shaped herald in third side panel; operating doors on all four bays; catalogue number appears on carton of cars sold separately; catalogued in 1958 only; replaced by Lionel's Alaska Hopper in 1959.

(A) No Lionel logo; found in early Lionel sets.   **10 15 50**

(B) 1/16" diameter Lionel logo near the ladder, just below herald in the third side panel; more difficult to find.   **10 15 50**

CRANES and DERRICKS

0860 DERRICK CAR 40' car; light gray, painted body; black lettering; "PENNSYLVANIA"; numbered "489711"; 1/16" diameter Lionel logo appears at the toolbox end of car; sidewalls and toolbox also finished in gray; black plastic derrick with fine metal link chain; sidewalls, toolboxes and derrick snap into holes in car floor; one brakewheel; derrick usually broken; catalogue number appears only on carton; catalogued in 1958 very difficult to find.   **15 20 50**

0879 UNION PACIFIC CRANE Red, painted cab; white lettering; "UNION PACIFIC" in white lettering; "03043" between the last door and end of cab, directly below the single smokestack; "Bucyrus Erie" appears at the roof line, next to the center cab door; 1/16" diameter Lionel logo appears on the cab skirt below the road number; unpainted black frame, roof access door and boom; boom operated with metal crank that came with car;

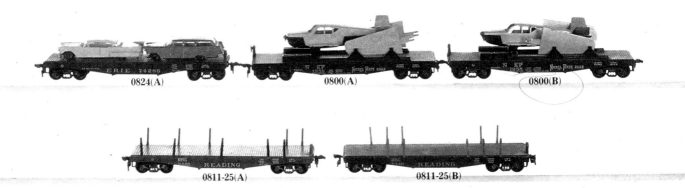

0824(A)   0800(A)   0800(B)

0811-25(A)   0811-25(B)

Athearn produced the Erie flatcar with automobiles as shown and in red. The Nickel Plate flatcars carry the two color variations of the airplane load

Both of the Reading cars illustrate the basic flatcar with ten steel stakes (brakewheels missing on these two).

two metal hooks and brass pulleys on boom; catalogued in 1958-60 and illustrated with the red, white and blue UP shield on the car frame, but not made this way; catalogue number appears on carton only; replaced in 1960 by Lionel's Illinois Central crane.

(A) Without Lionel logo; found in 1958 Lionel train sets.   20   30   55
(B) 1/16" diameter Lionel logo appears on the cab skirt below the road number.   20   30   55

CABOOSES

0817   MILWAUKEE   Silver, painted body; separate smokestack, hand-rails and additional details as found on other offset-cupola cabooses; black lettering; "MILWAUKEE ROAD" across body above windows; numbered "01924"; Lionel logo appears below grab-iron at cupola end; catalogue numbers appear on carton only; catalogued in 1958 only in set 5709; scarce.

(A) Semi-gloss paint finish.   10   15   40
(B) Flat finish.   10   15   40

0817-25   VIRGINIAN   Deep blue, painted body and roofwalk; unpainted black plastic floor, end platform and smokestack; separate brakewheels, wire handrails and stamped metal ladders; white lettering; "VIRGINIAN" appears below cupola; numbered "1217"; catalogued in 1958 only with set 5711; illustration shows "VIRGINIAN" appearing below the windows, but the car was never made this way; catalogue numbers appear on carton only; discontinued 1959.   20   25   60

0817-50   RIO GRANDE   Silver, painted body; black unpainted plastic end platform, smokestack and roofwalk; brakewheel at each end; wire handrails; stamped metal ladders; black lettering; "Rio Grande"; numbered "01439"; name and number appear within black pin stripes on side; 1/16" Lionel logo appears below grab-iron at end opposite cupola; catalogued in 1958 only in set 5715; Lionel did not sell the car in the gray and yellow scheme depicted in the catalogue illustration, however Athearn later sold that scheme in its own line.   15   20   35

0817-200   A.E.C.   Athearn shell; flat white, painted body and roofwalk; wire handrails; metal ladders; bright red lettering; "A.E.C.", "0817" and "BUILT BY LIONEL" appear on car side; "-200" suffix appears only in catalogue; catalogued in 1959 in set 5719; discontinued in 1960, then replaced in 1963 by Lionel's 0827-50.   15   20   35

0817-225   ALASKA   Athearn shell decorated by Lionel; painted dark flat blue; wire handrails; metal ladder; yellow lettering; "ALASKA" spelled across car side; illustration of Alaskan Boy appears between windows; "BUILT BY LIONEL" and "0817" also appear on car side; catalogued in 1959 only in set 5729; "-225" suffix appears only in catalogue; very rare.   10   20   55

0817-250   TEXAS SPECIAL   Athearn shell decorated by Lionel; painted bright red; wire handrails; metal ladders; white lettering; "BUILT BY LIONEL" and "0817" stamped on sides; "-250" suffix appears only in catalogue; very rare.   15   20   55

0817-275   NEW HAVEN   Painted flat black, with matching roofwalks; wire handrails; metal ladders; New Haven initials only, orange "N" and white

"H"; initials approximately 1/2" tall; catalogue number "0817" and "BUILT BY LIONEL" appear on side; catalogued in 1959 in set 5725 with the New Haven Rectifier; discontinued in 1960; this car is an Athearn shell decorated by Lionel; Lionel introduced its own model with the same catalogue number in 1963.   10   15   25

0817-300   SOUTHERN PACIFIC   Athearn shell decorated by Lionel; painted maroon body and roofwalk; two brakewheels; metal ladders; wire handrails; black unpainted plastic end platforms and frame; Lionel sprung trucks; yellow lettering; "SOUTHERN PACIFIC", "BUILT BY LIONEL" and "0817" appear on car side; no Lionel logo; catalogued in 1959 only in sets 5731 and 5717; in the illustration of set 5717, car is shown with black cupola, but it was not made that way; discontinued in 1960.

(A) With window inserts.   15   20   35
(B) Without window inserts.   15   20   35

WORK CABOOSES

0819-1   PENNSYLVANIA   Entire car, including roofwalks, painted dark gray; sprung metal trucks; wire handrails; metal ladder; black letter; "Maint." and "MW1741" appear on cab side; Lionel logo appears just above the grab-iron at the ladder end of cabin; catalogued in 1958 only; discontinued in 1959; very rare.   15   20   40

0819-25   U.S. NAVY   Painted light blue to match 51 U.S. Navy Switcher; black roofwalk, brakewheel and smokestack; metal ladder; wire handrails; white lettering; "U.S. NAVY" between cab windows; "1013" directly below road name; Lionel logo appears below the grab-iron at the ladder-end of car; catalogue number appears on carton only; catalogued in 1958 only; rare.   15   20   55

0819-50   WABASH   Light blue, painted body, toolboxes and cabin; unpainted black plastic roofwalk, brakewheel and smokestack; metal ladder; wire handrails; single brakewheel; white lettering; overscore and underscore enclose "WAB" and "615"; 1/16" Lionel logo appears between the grab-irons at the fence end of the car; catalogued in 1958 only in set 5707; illustration shows larger lettering than that which actually appears on car; discontinued in 1959.   15   20   55

0819-75   BALTIMORE & OHIO   Painted blue car body, cabin, toolboxes and fence; unpainted black plastic smokestack, brakewheel and roofwalk; single brakewheel at cabin end; "BALTIMORE & OHIO" above windows; large "B&O" between windows; "MWC17" below initials; Lionel logo appears by the grab-iron at the ladder-end of the car; no catalogue numbers on car; catalogued in 1958 only in set 5713; discontinued 1959.   15   20   35

0819-100   BOSTON & MAINE   Deep blue, almost purple, body, cabin, fence and toolboxes; black roofwalk, brakewheel and smokestack; metal ladder; wire handrails; white lettering; approximately 1/2"-square "B.M." logo between cabin windows; solid white "B" and white-outlined "M" comprise logo; road name appears below the windows; "MW24" below name; overscore and underscore enclose name and number; Lionel numbers appear on carton only; catalogued in 1958 as a separate item and in set 5717.

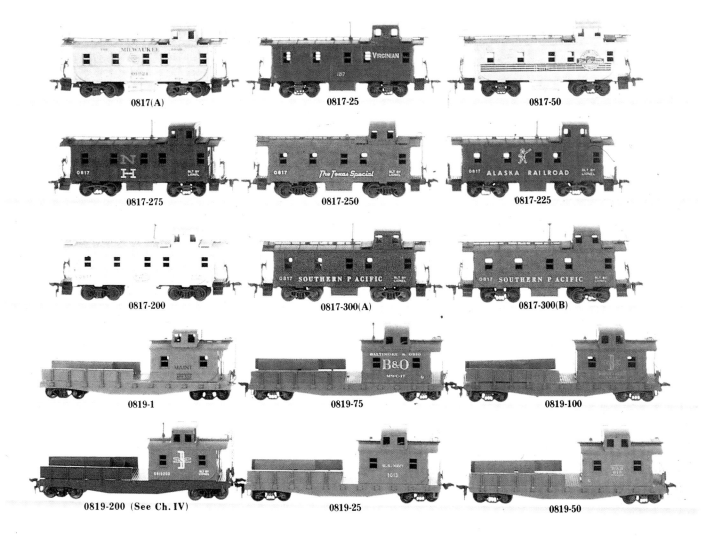

0817(A) 0817-25 0817-50

0817-275 0817-250 0817-225

0817-200 0817-300(A) 0817-300(B)

0819-1 0819-75 0819-100

0819-200 (See Ch. IV) 0819-25 0819-50

The cabooses shown on the top shelf were decorated by Athearn for Lionel, while those on the second and third shelves from the top are Athearn cabooses that were painted by Lionel. Produced in 1958 and 1959, the cabooses decorated by Lionel carry only part of their catalogue numbers on the car side. The five Athearn work cabooses are illustrated on the fourth and fifth shelf, along with with a factory error shown at left on the bottom shelf. This car has a cab manufactured and decorated by Lionel on an Athearn underframe.

This car was catalogued again in 1959 in sets 5723 and 5727; the former had the Athearn car, while the latter had 0819-200 from Lionel's production; the catalogue shows both cars with a two-color B.M. logo, but neither car was made this way.　　　　　　　　　　**15　20　35**

Chapter IV
From Hobbyline to Lionel Lines:
1959-1966

Sometime in 1958 Lionel approached John English, proprietor of Hobbyline, based in Morrisville, PA, and purchased the tooling from his company for $150,000.[1] By 1959 Lionel had reworked and put into service Hobbyline H0 scale model dies. In fact, Lionel purchased all of Hobbyline's dies, except for its passenger cars, which were acquired by Penn Line. In the mid-1950s, Hobbyline had catalogued a Fairbanks Morse locomotive and Madison-style passenger cars, but Lionel never produced these items—perhaps they too went elsewhere.

John English initially manufactured the A-5 Yardbird as a cast metal kit under the English trade name. Later, he manufactured the same locomotive as a plastic static model (illustrated) under the Hobbyline trade name. Lionel acquired the die work for this model in its deal with Hobbyline.

The 1959 catalogue shows a mixture of Lionel's new models and those made for Lionel by Athearn. The word "new" appears next to the catalogue entries for the Lionel items, and thus they can be distinguished from the remaining Athearn models. The catalogue introduced nine Alco diesels in three road names, two GP-9s, an electric, two steam locomotives, a diesel yard switcher, a snowplow and a motorized gang car. In addition to the many new locomotives, Lionel introduced sixteen pieces of rolling stock. Hobbyline's beautiful freight cars had fine quality sprung trucks similar to those used by Athearn, Globe and Varney. Two of the flatcars carried metal Matchbox models as loads. Track and transformers were also added, as were accessories, including a light tower, gateman, crossing gate and five plastic buildings. The buildings were actually Plasticville products packaged in Lionel boxes. The new Lionel drives were much like the band-driven units of 1958 and, in the authors' opinion, less dependable. A worm gear

was added to the drive, but rubber bands still operated as clutches, thus offsetting the advantage of the added gears. Six changes took place on the frames used for the Alcos, geeps and electrics in the eight years that Lionel produced the line. The motors and frames are listed separately from the locomotives, because body shells may be interchanged among mechanisms in some cases.

In addition to reworking Hobbyline dies, Lionel created its own dies for 1959. The Lionel dies produced models with thin plastic walls, while Hobbyline dies produced models with much heavier cross sections. The collector can distinguish models made in the Lionel dies from models made in the Hobbyline dies by examining the heaviness of the casting. Hobbyline dies were used for the new 0605 Yard Switcher, Alco diesel, tank cars, gondolas, flatcars, the new Alaska hopper cars and Lionel Corporation stamped boxcars.[2] The Texas Special sets (0704-0707) and tuscan Pennsylvania sets of passenger cars remained available from earlier Athearn production (until 1960, when Lionel began to produce its own cars).

It is interesting to note that many illustrations in the 1959 consumer catalogue depict Athearn pieces, such as the 0865 gondola with cannisters. The actual 1959 version produced by Lionel is a brown Hobbyline 40 foot gondola with Athearn cannisters. Numbered 0865-200, the gondola has gold lettering and five unmarked red cannisters—it can definitely be called "transitional!" Note that the catalogue tag-line "new" often appears next to items that have been available for at least a year.

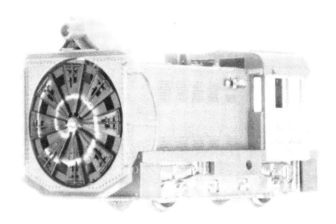

0561 Minneapolis & St. Louis Snowplow

Other pieces produced in 1959 include the new 0561 Minneapolis & St. Louis Rotary Snowplow with revolving

---

1. J. Sadorf, telephone call, January 27, 1985.

2. McComas & Tuohy, p. 105.

LIONEL HO CANADIAN PRICE LIST 1959

HO OUTFITS

5719	3 car AEC Switcher Frt. (4)	$26.95
5721	4 car Texas Special Frt. (4)	34.95
5723	4 car Steam Switcher Frt. (4)	39.95
5725	5 car New Haven Rectifier Frt. (4)	39.95
5727	5 car N. Y. Central GP-9 Frt. (4)	49.95
5717	6 car 4-6-2 Steam Frt. (4)	55.00
5729	5 car Alaskan "AB" w/Trestle Set (4)	55.00
5731	5 car 4-6-2 Steam Frt. w/Trestle Set (4)	69.95
5732	4 car Texas Spec. "ABA" 2 Motored Pass. (4)	69.95
5733	7 car S.F. "ABA" 2 Motored	82.50
	Fig. 8 Work Train (4)	

LOCOMOTIVES & MOTORIZED UNITS

0050	Gang Car NEW	10.95
0056	AEC Husky NEW	7.95
0560	Snow Plow	7.95
0561	Minn. & St. Louis Rotary Snowplow NEW	10.95
0565	Alco Santa Fe Powered "A" NEW	10.95
0566	Alco Texas Special Powered A NEW	10.95
0567	Alco Alaskan Powered "A" NEW	10.95
0570	Navy Yard Switcher	7.95
0591	New Haven Rectifier NEW	14.95
0596	N. Y. Central GP-9 NEW	14.95
0605	0-4-0 Steam Switcher NEW	14.95
0625LT	4-6-2 Steam Loco & Tender NEW	20.95

DUMMY B UNITS

0575	Alco Sante Fe NEW	4.95
0576	Alco Texas Special NEW	4.95
0577	Alco Alaskan NEW	4.95

DUMMY A UNITS

0586	Alco Texas Special NEW	5.75
0587	Alco Alaskan NEW	5.75
0595	Alco Santa Fe NEW	5.75

HO POWER PACKS

0100	2½ Amp. AC-DC Power Pack	21.50
0101	1¼ Amp. AC-DC Power Pack	14.95
0102	Fixed Voltage AC-DC Power Pack	25.00
0103	800 m.a. DC Power Pack NEW	10.95
0181	Cab Control	9.95
1144	75 Watt AC Power Supply	17.95

HO CARS

0704	Tex. Sp. Baggage Car w/Red Stripe NEW	5.75
0705	Tex. Sp. Pullman w/Red Stripe NEW	5.75
0706	Tex. Sp. Vista-Dome w/Red Stripe NEW	5.75
0707	Te. Sp. Observation w/Red Stripe NEW	5.75
0800	Flat Car w/Airplane	4.25
0801	Flat Car w/Boat	4.25
0805	A.E.C. Car w/Blinking Light NEW	5.75
0806	Flat Car w/Helicopter NEW	4.25
0807	Flat Car w/Bulldozer NEW	4.25
0808	Flat Car w/Tractor NEW	4.25
0814	4 Auto Transport Car	5.75
0815	Chemical Car	3.75
0817-275	N. H. Caboose NEW	3.75
0819-225	S. F. Work Caboose NEW	3.75
0824	Flat Car w/2 Autos	4.25
0830	Flat Car with 2 Vans	5.75
0834	Illum. Poultry Car NEW	5.75

HO CARS

0836	Alaskan Hopper NEW	3.75
0860	Derrick Car	5.75
0862	Gondola	2.95
0864-175	Timken Box Car	3.75
0864-300	Alaskan Box Car NEW	3.75
0864-325	D.S.S.A. Box Car NEW	3.75
0864-350	State of Maine Box Car	3.75
0865	Gondola w/Canisters	3.75
0866-200	Circus Car NEW	3.75
0870	Maintenance Car w/Generator NEW	4.25
0872-200	R'way Exp. Reefer NEW	3.75
0875	Flat Car w/Missile NEW	4.25
0879	Wrecker Crane	6.95
0880	Maintenance Car w/Light NEW	5.75

HO ACCESSORIES

0110	Graduated Trestle Set	5.75
0111	Elevated Trestle Set NEW	2.25
0114	Factory w/Horn	12.95
0117	Factory NEW	6.95
0118	Factory w/Whistle	15.95
0119	Landscaped Tunnel NEW	2.95
0145	Gateman NEW	7.95
0197	Radar Tower	7.95
0214	Girder Bridge	2.25
0252	Crossing Gate NEW	7.95
0310	Billboard Set NEW	1.50
0410	Surburban Ranch House Set NEW	1.50
0411	Figure Set w/Switchman's Shanty NEW	1.95
0412	Farm Set NEW	2.25
0413	Railroad Structure Set NEW	3.75
0414	Village Set NEW	4.50
0430	6 Tree Assortment NEW	1.50
0431	Landscape Set NEW	2.98
0494	Rotating Beacon NEW	7.95

HO TRACK & SWITCHES

0903	3" Straight Track	.35
0905	1½" Straight Track	.35
0906	6" Straight Track	.35
0909	9" Straight Track	.35
0983	3" Curved Track 18" Rad.	.35
0984	4½" Curved Track 18" Rad.	.35
0985	9" Curved Track 15" Rad.	.35
0986	4½" Curved Track 15" Rad.	.35
0989	9" Curved Track 18" Rad.	.35
0922	R. C. Switch Right Hand	5.95
0923	R. C. Switch Left Hand	5.95
0942	Manual Switch Right Hand	4.25
0943	Manual Switch Left Hand	4.25
0925	Straight Terminal Sec 9"	1.10
0919	Uncoupler-RE-Railer	1.50
0939	Uncoupling Unit Only	1.10
0950	RE-Railer Section	.98
0960	Bumper Track	.75
0975	Curved Terminal 18" Rad., 9" Long	1.10
0990	90° Crossover	3.25

REPLACEMENT LAMPS

L191	12V. Midget Cartridge Base	.50
L0214	12V. Midget Screw Base 1957 Locos	.50

This original Lionel HO Canadian price list from 1959 shows the higher dollar prices Canadian's paid due to import duties and the unfavorable exchange rate. According to Standard & Poor's Trade and Security Reference, the exchange rate of 1959 was $1.00 U.S. equals $1.043 Canadian.

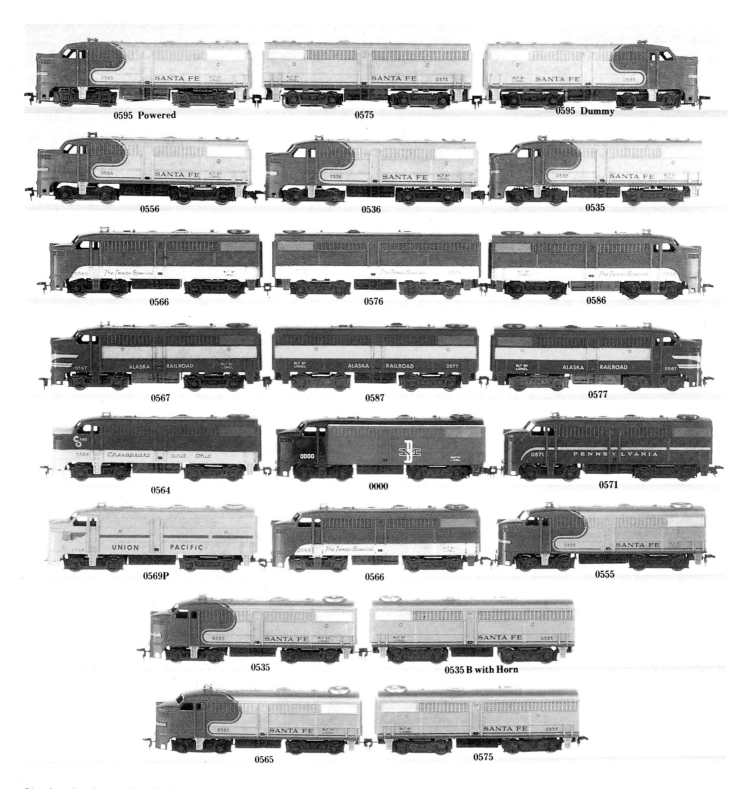

0595 Powered

0575

0595 Dummy

0556

0536

0535

0566

0576

0586

0567

0587

0577

0564

0000

0571

0569P

0566

0555

0535

0535 B with Horn

0565

0575

Lionel produced many Alco diesel locomotives with body shells made from old Hobbyline dies. The popular Santa Fe war bonnet paint scheme was offered with several catalogue numbers between 1959 and 1966. The Boston & Maine model shown on the fifth shelf is a factory prototype; this road name was not made for sale.

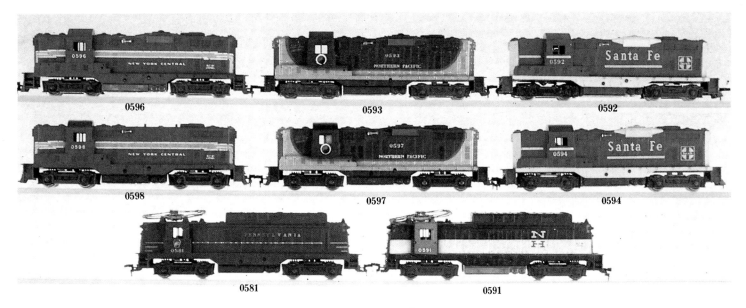

These are locomotives manufactured by the Lionel Corporation. The GP-9 shell was introduced in 1959. Lionel also created the die work for the Rectifier locomotive, which was introduced in 1958 with an Athearn mechanism and reissued in 1959 with a Lionel mechanism and new road names.

blade, a Lionel copy of Athearn's little Hustler locomotive, and the 0056 AEC Husky with headlight; both were produced with gear drives. The revolving blade on the 0561 was a separate, newly-made Lionel piece, too; Athearn no longer helped make these pieces after 1959. The 0591 New Haven Rectifier with pantograph had a band drive, as did the 0596 New York Central GP-9. The new 0625LT Pacific steam locomotive, still pictured with the Walschaerts valve gear that it never had, was a gear-driven work horse. The ex-Hobbyline Alco locomotives included A-B-A lash-ups decorated for the Santa Fe, Texas Special and Alaska Railroad. New in the accessory line were the 0050 Gang Car, 0145 Gateman and 0494 Rotary Beacon. A variety of Plasticville H0 buildings, girder bridges, billboards, trestles and the 0197 Rotary Antenna enabled enthusiasts to make their layouts into miniature replicas of larger 0 Gauge layouts.

By December of 1959 Lionel had made the transition from "early" H0, when manufacturing was contracted to outside suppliers, to the intermediate period when Lionel produced its own equipment based on its 0 Gauge heritage. No other manufacturer could boast of blinking 0805 AEC cars (the nuclear reactors in the cannisters glowed red), illuminated poultry cars, maintenance cars, circus cars, missile carrier flatcars or the prize of any Lionel H0 collection, the 0808 and 0807 flatcars with "Matchbox" series tractor and bulldozer, respectively. These were the only Lionel cars that ever had Matchbox models as loads. By 1960, the inventory of discontinued Athearn and Rivarossi items had been depleted.

BACK TO THE TINPLATE CONCEPT: 1960-1966

Josh Cowen once said, "after a kid watched a train go around more than three times, he would get bored with it, so give him plenty of action". Action is what the Lionel H0 line got in 1960. The new personnel in Roy Cohn's group made some radical changes. Emphasis on scale quality, as seen with Rivarossi and Athearn gave way to emphasis on the familiar "toy quality" and "play value" associated with Lionel trains. The 1960 consumer catalogue announced with fanfare, "A first in H0—Brand New Action Packed Operating Cars." 1960 was the

year of the 0319 Operating Helicopter Car, 0847 Exploding Target Car, 0850 Missile Launching Car, 0300 Operating Lumber Car and the 0301 Coal Dump car. There is a picture of the Lionel S.P. Helicopter Launch prototype in the March 1960 issue of **Railroad Model Craftsman**.

From 1960 through 1966 the H0 line failed miserably, especially the military items. According to Lenny Dean, "The new strategy was to get as much of the younger, mass-market railroaders as they could to join the model railroading ranks. Then eventually, as they grew up with Lionel trains, the H0 line would get more sophisticated as the line flourished." Apparently, Roy Cohn's objective was to get kids interested in H0 trains. "They were the future of Lionel," Dean stated.[3]

Hobbyists scoffed at the new Lionel toy trains designed for play value, but today collectors find the ingenious operating locomotives, cars and accessories to be very vital, exciting pieces. Lionel engineers almost literally shrank 0 Gauge operating cars to H0 proportions. Many of the items produced from 1960 to 1966, such as the Sheriff and Outlaw Car, Operating Milk Car and Giraffe Car operate just as well as the 0 Gauge counterparts. Many of these items display a sense of humor unique to Lionel, while others exhibit remarkable technological advances.

It is interesting to note that between 1959, when Roy Cohn assumed operational control of Lionel, and 1963 when he left, the Lionel Corporation lost $14 million.[4] During these years of corporate turmoil, trains, as a toy, were losing their popularity. Ultimately, the 0 Gauge line suffered and the fledgling H0 line, expecially the gimmick items, met disaster. Lionel also lost the H0 enthusiast market. "How would you like a car to explode on a trestle bridge, handmade out of toothpicks that it took you four years to build?" queries one collector interviewed by McComas and Tuohy.[5]

---

3. Phone interview with L. Dean, July 1984

4. McComas & Tuohy, ibid.

5. Ibid, p. 107

"The Father and Son Set", 225W, was heralded as one of the Lionel star performers in the 1960 advance catalogue. A product of the company's play-value marketing strategy, the set contained in two separate boxes identical "Super 0" and H0 sets. Some collectors call it the "over and under" set. While the components may be found for sale individually, the boxed set would be a very highly prized piece. The very rare 6357-50 Santa Fe red caboose came with the 0 Gauge portion of this set; the 0817-150 Santa Fe H0 caboose matches it.

1961

The 1961 H0 line continued to sell play action. New were 15 different train sets. The 0635LT Pacific became the new steam engine with headlight and smoke. The 0545 GE-44 Switcher with headlight and the 0602 Switcher with gear drive were also added, while the 0605 Saddle Tank locomotive remained in the line. A new four-wheel Canadian Pacific Husky 0054 appeared at the Toy Fair, though Lionel never made it for the U.S. market. Madison Hardware listed the piece on page 61 of their **Railroad Model Craftsman** ad in December 1961, but few if any seem to have been made. The Lionel Service Manual lists the piece and notes, "no ornamental horn 1-62. Body assembly is $1, but there is no bin number." Perhaps Lionel made only a few mock-ups or a short production run for the Canadian market; additional information requested.

The new H0 rolling stock for 1961 included the 0366 Operating Milk Can Unloading Car, 0333 Operating Satellite Launching Car, 0337 Animated Circus Giraffe Car and the 0039 Motorized Track Cleaning Car. H0 accessories included the 0068 Executive Inspection Car which has a sedan shell similar to the body found on the 0 Gauge 6414 Auto Car. The 0480 Missile Firing Range continues the military-space theme along with the Exploding Target Car. The 0282 Gantry was another addition to the 1961 line. Today, it is particularly difficult to find unbroken.[6]

1962

The big news for 1962 was that Joe Bonanno had squeezed Lionel's 0/027 horn and whistle mechanisms down to H0 size. For 1962 Lionel's Pacific 0645 had smoke, headlight and whistle. The deluxe A-B unit also had an operating headlight and air horn. The biggest difficulty was retention of the authentic sound. Lionel also adapted the Mallory magnetic coupler to some of its H0 sets. A two-inch magnetic bar sat between the rails in the heart of the new uncoupling system. The Mallory coupler, while not sanctioned by the N.M.R.A., was a further development of the N.M.R.A. X-2f coupler, and was designed to couple with regulation N.M.R.A. couplers. A

special feature of the new Lionel Mallory magnetic coupler was the extra long lateral pin extending from the shank to facilitate easier uncoupling. The couplers are truck-mounted carry-overs from 1961. The 0771 Lionel trucks were packaged separately at $1.50 a pair.

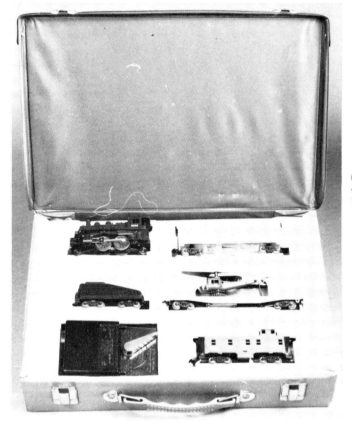

"Take me along" valise pack was a Lionel gimmick designed to create excitement and sales. "Have valise...will travel" touted the 1961 catalogue. The set came with a 0642LT Steam Locomotive and Tender, the 0337 Giraffe Car, 0319 Operating Helicopter Car, 0841 unmarked caboose; eleven sections of 0989 18" radius track, one section 0975 18" radius curved terminal section, 0103 power pack, 5767-15 carrying case, wires, instruction sheets and a 1961 pulp paper catalogue. Very rare, this set can bring as much as $300.00 in mint condition.

Other items representing the 1962 line are the 0370 Animated Sheriff and Outlaw Car, the 0845 Gold Bullion Car and the 0357 Cop and Hobo Car. The Cop and Hobo Car is a scaled-down reproduction of the 0 Gauge model. Every time the car rolls under a special trestle section a hobo and policeman jump on and off the car from the trestle. There is also a 0365 Minuteman Missile Launching Car and a 0349 Turbo Missile Firing Car. Indeed, these models reflect Lionel's ongoing desire to reproduce the highly imaginative 0 Gauge cars. According to Hal Carstens "model auto racing sets seemed to take some of the spotlight away from model trains that year, but it would take Lionel four more years to call it quite with the H0 line and eight more years to sell out their declining 0 train line," and discontinue train production altogether.[7]

---

6. Survey information adapted from **Railroad Model Craftsman**, May 1961, pp. 31-32.

7. **Railroad Model Craftsman**, May 1962, p. 18.

0602 0-6-0 STEAM SWITCHER WITH TENDER

0625LT PACIFIC WITH TENDER

Even the day before the New York Toy Fair opened, Lionel's Board Chairman, Roy M. Cohn, showed great optimism. The executives at Lionel felt that both H0 and 0 were going strong, with promise of steady growth in the future. (Cohn, Joshua Lionel Cowen's nephew, was better known for his role in the McCarthy hearings.)

1963

The performance of the H0 trains continued to improve as Lionel replaced rubber band-driven locomotives with newer models that featured a Helic drive (with a sprung steel band). The newer models included the 0571P Pennsylvania Alco diesel with headlight, the 0569P Union Pacific and the 0536 Santa Fe Alco A-B multiple unit. Steam locomotives improved, too. The 0636 Pacific steam locomotive with headlight and smoke received a new gear ratio for smoother operation. The 0595 Santa Fe dummy A, 0575 B unit and the new Santa Fe powered A unit with headlight and Helic drive are pictured in the catalogue as EMD F-3 or F-7 units, but they were actually produced as models of Alco diesels. In the GP-9 series, Lionel added the 0593P Northern Pacific powered unit, 0593T Northern Pacific dummy and the 0594P Santa Fe. Both of the powered units feature dual front headlights.

In retrospect, the cover of Lionel's 1963 Catalogue, which shows two model race cars and a train in an apparent race, seems quite appropriate. Eight pages at the rear of the catalogue describe motor racing sets. The fad had hit hard, and trains had fallen from popularity. Lionel attempted to follow the changes in the marketplace by offering its own race sets. Ironically, Lionel had created the first toy racing sets in 1912, long before the market desired such automotive toys.

0626LT PACIFIC WITH TENDER

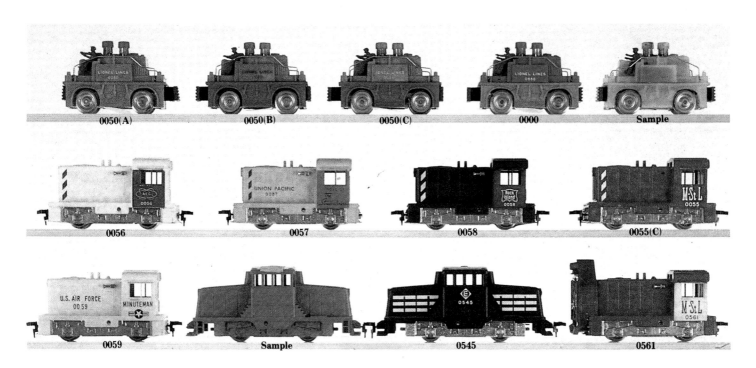

| 0050(A) | 0050(B) | 0050(C) | 0000 | Sample |

| 0056 | 0057 | 0058 | 0055(C) |

| 0059 | Sample | 0545 | 0561 |

A selection of small motorized units made by Lionel. The fourth gang car on the first shelf is a factory prototype, while the fifth seems to be an unpainted production sample. The unpainted 44 ton switcher, from the V. Rosa Collection, is also a factory prototype.

Many of 1962's operating cars were continued in 1963. The only new 1963 items are the 0815-85 Lionel Lines Chemical Car and the Boston & Maine boxcar. It is interesting to note that the 0864-400 B&M Boxcar is listed in the 1960, 1961 and 1963 catalogues. It is described as a new item in both 1960 and 1963, though it had the same number each year and no apparent change in design. The 1960-1961 car belongs to the early Lionel/Hobbyline group of boxcars. The 1963 car, we believe, is similar. It is in 1965 that the catalogue shifts to a new number, the 0874-60, although there is no reference to anything being new. This Lionel car is a cheapened version of the earlier Lionel/Hobbyline boxcar. It is smaller in height and very plain. It has a 6464-style steel plate on the bottom. The 0874-60 was also listed and, for the first time, illustrated in the 1966 catalogue.[8]

The 1962 0864-900 N.Y.C. boxcar was given a new number in 1963, without any indication of specific changes that may have been made. The hyphenated number most likely indicates that changes took place in either the truck or coupler design. The same car was renumbered 0874 in 1964, when Lionel began to replace the Hobbyline boxcars with a cheaper line of steel bottom cars. The 0874 N.Y.C. reappears in the 1965 and 1966 catalogues; again without reference to any changes.[9]

Another interesting piece of rolling stock released in 1963 is the 0827 Illuminated Safety First Caboose, while the 0845 Gold Bullion Transport, 0810 Emergency Generator Transport Car, 0805 Illuminated Radioactive Waste Disposal Car, 0889 Illinois Central Crane and 0813 Mercury Capsule Carrying Car are the premier pieces of collectible rolling stock produced in this year. The Northern Pacific 0593T and 0593P are very hard to find in new condition, while the 0571 Pennsylvania diesel and the 14163 four-unit Pennsylvania diesel passenger set are both extremely rare.

1964

By 1964, Lionel had begun to print its catalogue on a less-expensive, uncoated paper, yet the new catalogue devoted six pages to selling the H0 line. With the return of the 0 Gauge 773 steam locomotive, Lionel seemed to be preparing to offer greater quality in its line. Apparently, the company wished to reduce emphasis on the lower-quality space age cars. The catalogue showed eight H0 sets, with gear driven steam and diesel locomotives. The locomotive range includes the 0055 Minneapolis & St. Louis Husky switcher with headlight, the 0594P Santa Fe GP-9 and a deluxe 0646LTS Pacific steam locomotive with tender and whistle. A three-unit Alco diesel with air horn could be substituted for the 0646LTS steamer in set 14310. Lionel pushed neither the H0 nor the 0 Gauge space age cars, although a stock of each remained in inventory. Motor cars and other toys were listed in separate catalogues.

1965

The number of H0 catalogue pages decreased to four in the unusual 1965 consumer catalogue. Only a year remained before Lionel would discontinue the line. The equipment selection included the same fourteen action cars that had been offered in 1964. The 0646LTS continued to be the premier steam locomotive, and, once again, Lionel erroneously depicted the 0595 dummy A and the 0536 A-B combination as EMD F-units, rather than correctly as Alcos. The train set themes all seemed to indicate a return to the traditional railroading concept. During the year, the company also produced the 0874-60 Boston and Maine, which was not illustrated in the

8. Comment by Jack Fulton; verified by V. Rosa; March 4, 1984.
9. Ibid.

Hobbyline body (top shelf) and Lionel 0605 with drive mechanism. Note the raised portion of the boiler just ahead of the cab on the Lionel version. This bulge allowed room for Lionel's large motor.

catalogue, the 0646LTS Pacific with smoke and whistle, the 0626 without smoke or whistle and a 0595-0536 Santa Fe Alco with diesel horn. The 0626 is one of the rarest Lionel Pacifics of the late corporation run; this locomotive has a piston in its steam chest, although it is not equipped with a smoke unit.

1966

This was the last year of H0. Lionel showed five complete sets in the catalogue, but none of them was a dynamic offering. The Pacific steam with smoke and whistle became 0647LTS. The Sante Fe A-B combination with the diesel horn became 0537; the dummy A 0595. Lionel also produced the 0592 GP-9, which had direct-gear drive. The operating cars and space cars prevailed, most likely due to the large quantities remaining in inventory. The era for bobbing giraffes, guided missiles, helicopters and see-through gold bullion cars had crested, and Lionel management threw in the towel, thus surrending their

battle in the H0 market. Lionel filled all of its H0 orders from inventory in 1967.

LIONEL STEAM LOCOMOTIVES 1959-1966

With only small changes in their shells, all of the steam locomotives produced by Lionel were made from old Hobbyline dies. Locomotive shells and tender bodies were molded in black plastic. Locomotives had cast metal frames, while most tenders had sheet metal floors. All of the locomotives were lighted; some had smoke and whistle units. None of the locomotives were very powerful, because Lionel used the three-pole motor found in diesel units with worm gear drive. Current was collected by wipers that rubbed against the drive wheels. Wire handrails were applied to all Pacific locomotives. Sprung trucks were used on the tenders until 1963, after which solid frame trucks were used. Along with the change to solid frame trucks came minor changes in couplers and covers.

Introduced in 1961, the first smoke unit worked well considering its simplicity. It had a cast metal steam chest with an integral electric heating element. The unit used liquid to produce smoke, which was forced up the stack by a piston in the left side of the steam chest. The piston operated directly off the drive rod, which was stamped steel. Three plastic pouches of smoke fluid came with each locomotive. The whistle units were introduced in 1962 in the 0645 Pacific. The metal floor of the tender was replaced by a small plate fastened to the front of the tender. The truck fastened to the bottom of this plate, and the relay for the whistle was attached at the top. The rear truck was fastened directly to a plastic lug that was cast into the tender body. These trucks were the same type used on the later passenger cars made by Lionel. They were insulated with plastic wheels on one side. The motor for the whistle was the same type used on the Husky locomotives and was mounted vertically in the center of the tender with the whistle housing attached to the top shaft. A special button came with the locomotive to activate the whistle. A maintenance folder providing the "how to" on lamp change and lubrication came with each locomotive equipped with smoke and whistle units. All of the steam locomotives with these ingenious accessories are difficult to find.

Gd Exc Mt

0602 0-6-0 STEAM SWITCHER WITH TENDER Painted flat black; white lettering; "0602" on cab side; "PENNSYLVANIA" on side of slope-back tender; cast metal frame; 1960-type motor; plastic pilot and steam chest; valve gear includes wire guides, main rod and drive rods; "LIONEL" appears on gear cover plate; cast-on handrails; two headlights,

0635LT PACIFIC WITH TENDER

41

0636LTS PACIFIC WITH TENDER

0637LTS PACIFIC WITH TENDER

one with a bulb in boiler front and one dummy fixture above it; shell fastened to frame by one tab at the rear of frame and a screw passing through the smokestack; metal floor on tender; four-wheel metal tender trucks secured with screws to plastic studs extending from body casting through tender floor; catalogued in 1960 only; second most difficult to find of the steam switchers.   **40   60   75**

0605 TANK-TYPE STEAM SWITCHER Painted flat black; "0605" in white numerals appears below the cab window; no lettering appears anywhere on the unit; cast-on handrails and steps; lighted; combination cast metal and plastic frame; plastic pilot and steam chest; shell mounts to frame with two tabs at the end of frame, which pass through shell, and a screw passing through the smokestack into a weight at the front of frame; rear steps often broken after servicing; combination band and worm drive; easily bent side and drive rods made of very thin metal; coupler with top pivot pin used with metal cover; catalogued in 1959 for separate sale and in set 5723; catalogued again in 1960 for separate sale and in set 5737; available separately again in 1961-62; the only tank locomotive Lionel produced.
(A) 1959 motor.   **40   60   75**
(B) 1960 motor; different coupler.   **40   60   75**

0625LT PACIFIC WITH TENDER Painted flat black locomotive and tender shells; short tender with high sides; white lettering; catalogue number on cab side; "SOUTHERN PACIFIC" across tender side; wire handrails; headlight; cast metal frame, pilot and steam chest; no smoke unit; cast weight screwed to frame; frame lettered "LIONEL N.Y., N.Y."; cast metal pony and trailing trucks with plastic wheels; nylon gear drive; stamped metal drive rods; sprung metal trucks on tender; catalogued separately in 1959-61 and in sets 5717 and 5731 (1959) and sets 5745 and 5771 (1960).
(A) 1959 motor with ball bearings; motor secured by black plastic gear box cover.   **45   70   75**
(B) 1960 motor with thrust plate; motor fastened to frame with a single screw; sold in 1960-61.   **45   70   85**

0626LT PACIFIC WITH TENDER Flat black body and tender shell; white lettering; catalogue number appears on cab side; "SOUTHERN PACIFIC" on tender side; white stripe on boiler walkway; internally similar to 0625LT(B); slower gear ratio; no smoke unit, but locomotive does have a piston in the steam chest; thumb screw in stack secures shell; catalogued separately 1963-65 and in sets 14153 (1963) and 14270 (1964); very rare.

0642 2-4-2 STEAM SWITCHER WITH TENDER

0645LT PACIFIC WITH LONG HAUL WHISTLING TENDER

0646LTS PACIFIC WITH LONG HAUL WHISTLING TENDER

(A) Painted shell; 1963.   60 85 125
(B) Unpainted shell; 1964-65.   60 85 125

0635LT PACIFIC WITH TENDER Painted flat black; white lettering; catalogue number on cab side; "SOUTHERN PACIFIC" on tender side; internally similar to 0625LT(B); heating element in top portion of steam chest; plastic piston located in left side of chest to force smoke up the stack; larger smokestack hole for thumb screw to fasten shell to frame; stamped metal valve guides; catalogued separately in 1961-62 and in sets 5756 with three tuscan Athearn passenger cars, 5757, 5762 (1961) and in 14043 (1962).

                                             50 70 90

0636LTS PACIFIC WITH TENDER Flat black, painted body and tender shell; white lettering; catalogue number on cab side; "SOUTHERN PACIFIC" on tender shell; white stripe on boiler walkway; with smoke unit; very similar to 0635LT; short tender with solid frame trucks; catalogued 1963-66; not easily found in good condition.   70 85 90

0637LTS PACIFIC WITH TENDER Uncatalogued; painted flat black; white lettering; catalogue number on black paper sticker on cab side; "SOUTHERN PACIFIC" stamped on tender; white stripe along boiler walkway; turned brass bell (rather than molded plastic bell found on other Pacific shells); metal handrails with three cotter pins as stanchions;

handrails extend to pilot; smoke unit and headlight; frame marked "BUILT BY LIONEL"; geared axle visible through opening in frame; traction tire on one rear driver; short box-type tender; 1960-type motor; steel worm drive; 1963; rare.
(A) Painted shell.   70 80 100
(B) Unpainted shell.   70 80 100

0642 2-4-2 STEAM SWITCHER WITH TENDER Painted flat black; "0642" in white numerals appears below cab windows; tender matches that found with 0602, but it is unmarked; larger cast metal frame; plastic steam chest and gear cover; cast metal pilot; larger drive wheels; sheet metal lead and trailing trucks with plastic wheels; 1960-type motor; band and worm drive; separate drive and connecting rods found; Lionel name does not appear anywhere on locomotive; catalogued 1961 separately and in sets 5752 and 5767; catalogued again in 1962 separately and in set 14023; discontinued 1963.   35 50 65

0643 2-4-2 STEAM SWITCHER WITH TENDER Painted flat black; "0643" in white numerals appears below cab windows; very similar to 0642; sprung trucks replaced in favor of solid frame trucks; no connecting rods; Helic drive; unlettered tender; catalogued in 1963 only in set 14133; very scarce.   50 60 80

0647LTS PACIFIC WITH LONG HAUL TENDER

0645LT   PACIFIC WITH LONG HAUL WHISTLING TENDER   Black; white lettering; catalogue number on cab side; "SOUTHERN PACIFIC" on tender; no stripe on boiler walkway; similar to 0635LT, but two electrical wires extend from the rear of cab to whistle in tender; blackened wheels on locomotive; long haul tender; catalogued separately 1962-63 and in sets 14074 and 14098 (1961); scarce.   **60   90   120**

0646LTS   PACIFIC WITH LONG HAUL WHISTLING TENDER   Similar to 0645LTS; black; white lettering; catalogue number on cab side; "SOUTHERN PACIFIC" on tender; catalogued in one set 1963-65 and separately 1964-65; scarce.
(A) Silver wheels.   **60   90   120**
(B) Blackened wheels.   **60   90   120**

0647LTS   PACIFIC WITH LONG HAUL WHISTLING TENDER   Similar to 0637LTS, with addition of headlight and smoke unit; white catalogue number appears on black paper sticker on cab side; tender lettered "SOUTHERN PACIFIC"; solid-frame, six-wheel tender trucks; catalogued only in 1966, separately and in set 14300; the last steam locomotive produced.   **60   90   120**

DIESEL AND ELECTRIC LOCOMOTIVES

1959 FRAMES, MOTORS AND COUPLERS
(Used on 0593, 0596 and 0591)

1959 Geep and Rectifier Mechanism

When Lionel produced its first diesel locomotive mechanism, it attempted to combine features from the early Rivarossi gear-driven locomotives and the later belt-driven Athearn units. The hybrid mechanism worked so poorly that it only lasted one year in production.

The cast metal frame (part number 0596-16) has integral coupler pads with pins that project downward through the metal cover; two raised areas support the one-piece nylon drive shaft and pulley that connects the motor shaft with a rubber coupling, much the same as the 1958 Athearn units. Neoprene 0 rings transfer power from the double-shafted, three-pole motor to the cast metal trucks, both of which are powered. The motor, which sits on four raised areas in the well of the frame, is held together by a single screw. There is a socket for a bayonet-base headlight at each end. A single screw secures each truck to the frame. Blackened wheel sets on some units contribute to poor operation, because they impede current collection. In 1960 the Service Stations were instructed to change the blackened wheel sets to the newer nickel-plated brass wheel sets just introduced. The 1959 locomotives use a standard horn hook coupler.

1960 FRAMES, MOTORS AND COUPLERS

The 1960 frame is similar to the previous frame with the following exceptions: cavity beneath the motor on 1959 frames filled, two vertical extensions added to increase weight, larger nylon drive shaft with pulley; hole added to accept pin found on

1960 Geep and Rectifier mechanism with blackened frame, added weight and heavier drive shaft.

new coupler, nickel-plated wheel sets and improved electrical conductivity. The 1960 motors have sleeve bearings, two screws and interlocks bvetween the halves. Used on the 0581 Pennsylvania electric, 0597 NP GP-9 and 0598 NYC GP-9.

1963—FRAMES USED ON 0593 GP-9

1963 Helic drive Geep mechanism with same frame and motor as 1960 unit.

Identified as "Helic Drive" in the catalogue, the 1963 frame is fairly similar to that of 1960. Only one truck is powered. Lionel continued to use the double-shafted 1960 motor, although only one shaft transmitted torque to the powered truck with the new Helic spring drive belt. The trucks have cast metal sides and nickel-plated wheel sets. The 1963 couplers have a half-inch shank extending from one side. This coupler was also used on most rolling stock from 1963 to 1966. Both headlights remain from the 1960 design. There is no part number on the frame, but it is stamped "LIONEL N.Y., N.Y."

1965—FRAME USED ON 0594 SF GP-9

1965 mechanism with large motor and single gear/worm driven power truck.

In 1965, Lionel reintroduced the 1963 frame with a different drive train. The 1965 frame has a larger motor and a single truck with all-gear drive. A rubber coupling connects the motor shaft to the metal drive shaft of the truck. The truck is secured by a single pin that passes through the frame and the plastic truck housing. There is no part number on the frame, but it is stamped "LIONEL N.Y., N.Y."

1966—FRAME USED ON 0592 SF GP-9

1966 direct-drive mechanism with single power truck. We believe that this mechanism was used only on the 0592 Santa Fe of 1966.

Lionel modified the frame again in 1966 and added more weight to the center of the frame. The frame is solid metal from truck to truck. The rear axle of the cast metal rear truck is driven directly by the truck-mounted, 1960-type motor. The dummy front truck is all plastic. Headlights and couplers are similar to those on the 1965 frame. There is no part number on the frame, but it is stamped "BUILT BY LIONEL". Minor changes in gear ratios occurred during production.

ALCO DIESEL FRAMES

Dummy B unit frame with horn mechanism. Note the spring clips that hold the two AA-size batteries on the right side.

The development of Alco frames follows that of the Geep frames. However, the shape is different, because of the difference in body contours. Unlike the underside of a Geep frame, the area between the trucks on an Alco frame is more exposed to show the battery box and ladder detail. Alco frames have only one headlight, which is located at the front of the unit. The changes to nickel-plated wheel sets and blackened frames occurred in production of both the Alco and GP-9 locomotives. Dummy A units have the same frame as found on the powered models, while the B units usually have a plastic frame. Very few B units were made with a cast frame.

RECTIFIERS

0581 PENNSYLVANIA RECTIFIER Painted flat tuscan; keystone herald stamped on each end and cab sides; gold striping and lettering; "0581" on cab side; "PENNSYLVANIA" on hood; single stripe over entire length, broken by cab; two smaller stripes on front end, just below the longer stripe; brass pantograph; clear headlight lens at each end; part number inside shell; sold without handrails, although stanchion holes present; black 1960-type frame; catalogued in 1960 only as a separate item and in set 5742 with three Athearn Pennyslvania passenger cars.   **50   80   120**

0591 NEW HAVEN RECTIFIER Painted black; bright orange cab roof and cab sides; white "0591" on cab side; 1/2" wide white band along length of body, broken by cab; white "N.H." on each end; larger logo, with white "N" and orange "H" on long hood; orange "Built by Lionel" on white stripe; one brass pantograph; clear headlight lens at each end; only cab end lighted; sold without handrails, although stanchion holes are present; part number inside shell; decorated by Lionel; introduced in 1959 as a separate item and in set 5725; also listed, without illustration, in 1960.

(A) Flat black, painted body; 1959-type frame with natural steel finish.
   50   80   120

(B) Gloss black, painted body; blackened 1960-type frame.   **50   80   120**

EMD GP-7 AND GP-9 DIESELS

0592 SANTA FE GP-9 Painted medium blue body; bright yellow striping and lettering; "0592" on cab sides; yellow ends and dynamic brake housing; single stripe along floor line; "Santa Fe" on hood below brake housing; herald next to name; two metal horns; clear plastic lens at each end; only cab end lighted; catalogued only in 1966, separately and in 14260; set number used again in 1966 with different locomotive; rare with the proper gear-driven mechanism.   **35   60   80**

0593 NORTHERN PACIFIC GP-9 Similar to 0597, except "0593" appears on cab side; different frame than 0593; catalogued separately in 1963 and in set 14193 with dummy 0593T; the dummy appears in the catalogue with the number visible in the illustration; it was not produced with the "T" stamped on the model, however the "T" does appear in the catalogue and on the carton.   **35   60   80**

0594 SANTA FE GP-9 Similar to 0592, except "0594" appears on cab side; catalogued separately in 1963 and 1965, in set 14143 in 1964 and in set 14260 in 1965.   **30   60   80**

0596 NEW YORK CENTRAL GP-9 Painted dark gray; light gray band bordered by white pin stripes on side of long and short hoods; white lettering; "Built by Lionel" at the end of long hood; road name at center; two metal horns, one on the short hood and one just below the second fan on the side of the long hood; sold without handrails, although stanchion holes are present; 1959-type frame and drive; catalogued only in 1959 as a separate item and in freight set 5727; scarce.   **50   80   100**

0597 NORTHERN PACIFIC GP-9 Black and gold, painted body; red pin stripe between principal colors; gold "0597" and "NORTHERN PACIFIC" on long hood; decal herald on cab sides; red "Radio Equipped" on short hood; two metal horns; 1960-type motor and frame; catalogued in 1960 separately and in freight set 5743; catalogued again in 1961 separately and in set 14064; discontinued in 1963; scarce.   **40   60   80**

0598 NEW YORK CENTRAL GP-7 Similar to 0596, less roof-mounted dynamic brake housing; "0598" on cab side; 1960-type frame and motor; catalogued in 1961 separately and in freight set 5755; catalogued again in 1962 only as a separate item; more common than 0596.   **30   60   80**

ALCO DIESELS – POWERED A UNITS

Note: All of the Santa Fe Alcos were decorated in the red and silver war bonnet scheme. These units headed most passenger sets from 1959 until the end of production in 1966. They were all made from the old Hobbyline dies. With the exception of road numbers, markings are the same on all units. The forward portion of the body is red, while the roof and sides are silver. Black and yellow pin stripes separate the principal body colors. "Built by Lionel" appears in the last lower side panel; the road name appears at the center. All lettering is black. The catalogue number appears just behind the cab door on each side. Each shell has one clear headlight lens, two metal horns on the roof and a Santa Fe decal just below the headlight.

0535 SANTA FE See "Note"; catalogued in 1962 for separate sale with the 0535W D unit with horn, both units catalogued in set 14004, 1902-type frame; scarce.   **45   50   80**

0536 SANTA FE See "Note"; catalogued in 1963 for separate sale and with the 0535W B unit; also in set 14203 in an A-B-A combination; catalogued again in 1964-65 separately and in an A-B-A combination in set 14310.

(A) 1963-type frame; 1963-64.   **40   50   75**

(B) 1965-type frame; 1965 only.   **40 50 75**

0537 SANTA FE See "Note"; direct-drive rear truck with two traction tires; 0537 B unit also catalogued, but made as 0535W; A-B-A combination sold separately and in set 14310; rare with right drive unit.   **35 60 90**

0555 SANTA FE See "Note"; Helic drive; 1963-type frame; catalogued in 1963 separately and in set 14173 with four red-striped passenger cars; catalogued again in 1964 in set 14290; catalogued also in 1965 in set 14320; discontinued in 1966; rare.   **35 60 90**

0556 SANTA FE See "Note"; direct-drive rear truck; catalogued only in 1966 in set 14320 with 0575 dummy B unit; very rare.   **40 50 75**

0564 CHESAPEAKE & OHIO Painted dark blue; bright yellow cab hood and lower side panels; blue lettering; "C.O." on nose and on cab sides just below windows; "Built by Lionel" does not appear on model; two metal horns; clear headlight lens; 1960-type frame; catalogued in 1960 for separate sale and in a military set 5739; catalogued in 1961 separately and in set 5733; discontinued in 1962; no C & O dummy units were made.

                                   40 60 75

0565 SANTA FE See "Note" concerning Santa Fe units; 1959 catalogue incorrectly describes 0565 as a dummy A unit; catalogued again in 1960, for separate sale with 0575 dummy B unit and in set 5747 also with the B unit; catalogued again in 1961 in sets 5758 and 5759; catalogued again in 1963.

                                   40 50 75

0566 TEXAS SPECIAL Painted red body; white lower side panels from cab side below windows to rear of unit; white star below headlight; red lettering on white panels; two metal horns; catalogued in 1959 separately and in two sets; catalogued in 1960 in an A-B combination for separate sale and in set 5770; sold only in A-B combination in 1961 and in set 14054 in 1962; the most frequently catalogued road name after Santa Fe; all Texas Special passenger cars were produced by Athearn; very common.
(A) 1958/59-type frame; flat red.   **25 40 60**
(B) 1960-type frame; semi-gloss red.   **25 40 60**

0567 ALASKA Painted dark blue; deep flat yellow from cab door to rear of unit; road name decal on nose; blue lettering; "Built by Lionel", road name and number on yellow band in lower side panels; two metal horns; clear plastic headlight lens; 1959-type frame with natural zamac finish; catalogued in 1959 only in an A-B-A combination and in set 5729; rare.

                                   40 60 95

0568 UNION PACIFIC Painted semi-gloss yellow; thin gray stripe centered from just behind the cab door to rear of unit; red lettering; "UNION PACIFIC" and "0568" appear in the lower side panels; light gray UP winged herald just below cab windows; two metal horns; plastic headlight lens; 1960-type frame; catalogued in 1962 only in set 14033; no dummy units made in this road name; rare.   **50 75 100**

0569P UNION PACIFIC Similar to 0568, with new number; "P" does not appear with number on locomotive; "Built by Lionel" does not appear on this unit.
(A) 1962-type frame.   **40 60 80**
(B) 1963-type frame with Helic drive; two rubber tires.   **40 60 80**

0571 PENNSYLVANIA Unpainted maroon body; keystone herald decal below headlight on nose; 1/8" yellow stripe from rear of unit to cab side and down to floor; road name on lower side panels; number on cab side; "Built by Lionel" does not appear on this unit; 1963-type frame with Helic drive and two rubber tires; catalogued in 1963 only, as a separate item and in passenger set 14163; no dummy units made in this road name; very rare.

                                   60 90 120

ALCO DIESELS — DUMMY A and B UNITS

The Dummy units were not made in all road names. Lionel had proposed many different road names (see photographs of B-unit prototypes), but the lack of sufficient advance orders preempted several schemes. All A units have a headlight; one B unit has a horn.

0535 SANTA FE Dummy B unit with horn; similar to 0575; battery-powered horn; metal truck side frames; 1963-type plastic frame; horn performs poorly; catalogued in 1962 in sets and in an A-B combination;

continued in many combinations through 1966; difficult to find with horn intact.   **30 45 75**

0575 SANTA FE Dummy B; silver, painted body; red, yellow and black striping; lettering as found on A units; plastic trucks screwed in place; no light; catalogued 1959-63 and 1965-66.
(A) Cast metal frame.   **10 15 25**
(B) Plastic frame.   **10 15 25**

0576 TEXAS SPECIAL Dummy B unit; painted red body; white stripe; road name, number and "Built by Lionel" on white stripe; catalogued in sets and separately 1959-61; common.
(A) Cast metal frame.   **10 15 25**
(B) Plastic frame.   **10 15 25**

0577 ALASKA Dummy B unit; painted and lettered per A unit; numbered "0577"; 1959 plastic frame; catalogued in 1959 only separately and in set 5729; rare.   **25 40 75**

0586 TEXAS SPECIAL Dummy A unit; painted and lettered like powered unit; numbered "0586"; 1958-type metal frame; blackened wheels; catalogued only in 1959 as a separate item.   **25 45 75**

0587 ALASKA Dummy A unit; similar to powered A unit, but numbered "0587"; 1959-type metal frame; catalogued in 1959 only as a separate item; rare.   **20 25 35**

0595 SANTA FE Dummy A unit; similar to powered A unit, but numbered "0595"; 1959-type metal frame; blackened wheels; catalogued in many sets and in multiple-unit combinations; catalogued 1959 and 1961-66; very common.   **10 15 20**

SMALL MOTORIZED UNITS

With the exception of the Gang Car, which has a sheet metal frame, all of the four-wheel diesels have a cast metal frame with direct gear drive to both axles. They can be found with either brass or nylon worm gears on the motor shafts. Similar to the design used for Alco frames, the two halves are secured by two screws; the motor is held in place between the halves, one of which is insulated. The bracket for the single headlight is held in place by one of the coupler-mounting screws. The frame is not an Athearn product, as some people believe. Rather, it is a Lionel item, which was introduced in 1959 and continued through 1966. A black plastic nameplate, which bears the Lionel name in white letters, is located between the two wheel sets. The plate also serves to seal the motor and gears from dust and dirt. It is found on all Husky switchers. All of the small diesel units are scarce.

0050(A)

0050 SECTION GANG CAR Unpainted plastic body; metal handrails; stamped metal frame; nickel-plated brass wheels as found on Alco diesels;

blue rubber man; blue rubber bumpers; "Lionel Lines" and "0050" on side; shaft motor drives 0 ring, which drives axles; reverses when either bumper contacts a solid object; runs fairly well; catalogued 1959-63.

(A) Orange body; white lettering; 1959-60.   20   40   75
(B) Orange top; gray bottom; black lettering; 1961.   20   40   75
(C) Similar to (B), but white lettering; 1962.   20   40   75
(D) Gray top; orange bottom; white lettering; 1963.   30   50   100

0055 M.St.L. Husky; painted red; white trim at front of the hood; white lettering; road name and number on cab side; illustrated in the black and white catalogues with white cab sides, but not produced as shown; headlight; catalogued in sets and separately 1961-66; catalogued more than any other small locomotive.

(A) 1960-type frame with brass worm gear; two metal horns.   25   40   60
(B) Later frame with nylon worm gears; two metal horns.   25   40   60
(C) Similar to (B), but no horns; 1964-66.   25   40   60

0056 A.E.C. Husky; painted white body; red cab sides; red trim on front edge of hood; white lettering; "A.E.C." and "0056" on cab sides; clear lens at each end; operating headlight at front only; two metal horns; body shell as manufactured by Lionel may be differentiated from Athearn product, as the Lionel unit has a much larger headlight housing; also, Athearn units have "HUSKY" molded into front radiator, Lionel units do not; 1959-type motor; catalogued in 1959 in set 5719 and separately in 1959-60; scarce.

(A) Regular version, as described.   35   60   90
(B) Promotional model for NBC; painted and lettered as regular version; decal with "WNBC-660 N.Y." in black letters on side of hood; model displayed on desk-top display with a left-hand track switch, three short sections of track and a bumper; a plaque on the front of the display is lettered "NATIONAL BROADCASTING COMPANY"; a plaque on the end is lettered "MADE BY/THE LIONEL CORPORATION"; the top of the display is lettered to indicate changes in the names of the N.Y. television and radio stations; may be one of a kind; T. Shepler Collection.   **NRS**

0057 UNION PACIFIC Husky; painted yellow; gray cab sides; red lettering and trim on front edge of hood; road name and number on side of hood; two metal horns; headlight lens inserts; 1959-type motor; catalogued in 1960 only for separate sale; very scarce.   40   60   90

0058 ROCK ISLAND Husky; flat black, painted body; bright red cab sides; white lettering; road name and catalogue number on cab side; white trim on front edge of hood; two metal horns; headlight lens inserts; 1960-type frame; catalogued in set 5735 in 1960 and as a separate item from 1960 to 1963, when it was discontinued.

(A) Brass worm gear.   25   40   60
(B) Nylon worm gear.   25   40   60

0059 U.S. AIR FORCE Husky; painted white; blue and red Air Force herald on cab side; dark blue lettering; "MINUTEMAN" on cab side; two metal horns; headlight lens inserts; 1960-type frame with brass gears; catalogued only in 1962 for separate sale; second rarest of the Husky locomotives.   50   80   100

0068 EXECUTIVE INSPECTION CAR

0068 EXECUTIVE INSPECTION CAR Painted red body; light gray unpainted bumpers at front and rear; clear plastic one-piece window insert; white sidewalls stamped on the four cast-on wheels; two holes in the bottom of car doors mount shell to Husky frame; no couplers nor lights; no lettering nor numbers on body; catalogued for separate sale only in 1961-62; shown in 1962 catalogue with "7" on its door; the body shown was made for the

Lionel race car sets of the same year; it does not have the holes for mounting on the Husky mechanism.

(A) Frosted windows.   45   75   100
(B) Clear windows; T. Shelper Collection.   **NRS**

0545 ERIE LACKAWANNA GE 44 ton switcher; black, painted body; white lettering; road number and large diamond herald on side; white grid trim; one working headlight; cast-on steps and couplers at each end; only four-wheel diesel with body-mounted couplers; 1959-type motor and frame; catalogued in 1961 separately and in set 5751; catalogued in 1962 separately and in set 14013.   35   50   75

0561 M.St.L. SNOW BLOWER Husky; bright red, painted body; white cab sides; red lettering; road name and number appear on cab sides; design similar to that of the 0 Gauge snow blower; red blower housing; black plastic plow blade; operates by metal shaft and rubber cap driven directly by the motor shaft; solid plastic headlight fixture cast onto top of blower housing; no headlight bulb or fixture; 1959-type motor; rear coupler only; catalogued as a separate item 1959-60; rarest Husky.   70   90   125

PASSENGER CARS—BUILT BY LIONEL 1961-1966

The cars produced with new Lionel tooling are models of streamlined cars with fluted sides and roofs made by the Budd Company of Philadelphia. All of the cars have heavy plastic shells. There are two main castings: one with the sides, ends and floor, the other with roof and windows. The illuminated cars have four-wheel metal trucks which are insulated on opposite sides. The light bulbs are secured to a copper strip that is fastened to the car floor, and current flows from the trucks to the copper strip through the fluted metal truck pin. A third pin at the center of the car also fastens the strip in place. Each car side has a smooth surface around and immediately above the windows; there are three smooth number boards in the fluted area. These were used for any striping or lettering that appeared on the cars. There are only two road names in the series, Santa Fe and Pennsylvania. These lighted cars are readily identified by locating the central hole for the pin that secures the lighting strip. All of these cars are scarce.

0712 SANTA FE BAGGAGE CAR Semi-gloss silver finish; red lettering; catalogue number and road name appear on two or three of the molded letterboards; third board is always blank; frosted windows; catalogued in 1961 in set 5759, in 1962 in set 14108, in 1963 in set 14173; no baggage cars were made available after 1964.

(A) Heat-stamped red stripe above windows; illuminated.   15   20   30
(B) Similar to (A), no lights.   15   20   30
(C) No stripe; no lights.   15   20   30

0713 SANTA FE PULLMAN Semi-gloss silver finish; red lettering; catalogue number and road name on car side; road name on center panel; frosted windows; catalogued in the same sets as noted for 0712; also available 1963-64. See also 0733, which has "0713" on the car side.

(A) Heat-stamped red stripe above windows; illuminated.   15   20   30
(B) Similar to (A), no lights.   15   20   30
(C) No stripe; no lights.   15   20   30

0714 SANTA FE VISTA DOME Semi-gloss silver finish; red lettering; clear plastic dome; dozen red passenger seats visible through dome; catalogued with other striped cars in same sets; discontinued in 1964; much more difficult to find than other Santa Fe cars.

(A) Heat-stamped red stripe above windows; illuminated.   20   25   35
(B) Similar to (A), no lights.   20   25   35
(C) No stripe; no lights.   20   25   35

0715 SANTA FE OBSERVATION Semi-gloss silver finish; red lettering; catalogued like the foregoing Santa Fe cars; more easily found than the 0712 or 0714. See also 0735, which has "0715" on the car side.

(A) Heat-stamped red stripe above windows; illuminated.   15   20   30
(B) Similar to (A), no lights.   15   20   30
(C) No stripe; no lights.   15   20   30

0723   0725

0723 **PENNSYLVANIA PULLMAN CAR** Tuscan lettering; no lighting; four-wheel metal trucks; catalogued in 1963 in set 44163, and again in 1964-65.

(A) Silver body; tuscan roof; clear window insert; 1964; rare. **30 45 60**

(B) Silver body and roof; frosted window insert; 1965-66. **15 30 40**

0725 **PENNSYLVANIA OBSERVATION CAR** Tuscan lettering; no lighting; four-wheel metal trucks; catalogued in 1963 in set 44163, and again in 1964-65.

(A) Silver body; tuscan roof; clear window insert; 1964; rare. **30 45 90**

(B) Silver body and roof; frosted window insert; 1965-66. **15 20 25**

0733 **SANTA FE PULLMAN** Painted silver; tuscan lettering; car numbered "0713", although catalogue number differs due to change in color of lettering; no stripe; no lights; four-wheel metal trucks; catalogued in 1964 in set 14290, which had two Pullmans because the Vista Dome and baggage were unavailable, and in different sets 1965-66; scarce. **20 25 30**

0735 **SANTA FE OBSERVATION CAR** Similar to 0733; car numbered "0715", rather than "0735"; catalogued like 0733; scarce. **20 25 30**

LIONEL BOXCARS

The early boxcars introduced by Lionel are all products of the old Hobbyline dies. They have thick plastic shells and oversized detail in the casting. They are all rather high in profile. The cars are assembled from four separate pieces, with the roof and top door guide being one casting, the floor, sides and ends as another and a separate door on each side. They have sprung trucks, which are screwed in place. Most of the cars were catalogued for only one year, but a few of the cars reappeared with different numbers for several years. Few of the cars were catalogued in sets.

Towards the end of production in 1964, there were a few boxcars made from a new Lionel die. These cars are few in number and very different in appearance from the earlier cars. They have much lighter shells, with a thinner section and a lower profile. Lionel continued to use operable doors, but the later cars had a claw foot-style door, which was easily

damaged. They have metal floors; some have black plastic floor bracing beneath the floor detail. Others have a metal floor with only a plastic bolster to hold the trucks. All of these cars have plastic talgo-type trucks. Produced for only two years, the later style boxcars are more difficult to find than the Hobbyline types.

0864-275 **STATE OF MAINE** Similar to 0864-350, except number "0864-275" appears on car instead; catalogued in 1962 only. **25 35 40**

0864-300 **ALASKA** Painted dark blue to match the Alaska Alco diesels; 1/4" yellowish-orange band on the side; yellow lettering; catalogue number and outline of the Alaskan Boy appears to the left of the door; road name spelled at right; "Built by Lionel" on car side; all detail molded into body casting, including floor bracing, brakes and valves; five-board door; sprung metal talgo-type trucks; "LIONEL" on cast floor; weighted with a metal slug above each truck; one of the first three boxcars introduced by Lionel; 1959 only. **30 40 50**

0864-325 **D.S.S.A.** Painted red body; matching door; flat black roof; white lettering; "Built by Lionel" on car side; sprung trucks; molded detail as described for 0864-300; catalogued in one set in 1959, 5725, and as a separate item from 1959 until 1961; second of the H0 boxcars.
24 30 40

0864-350 **STATE OF MAINE** Painted red, white and blue; white lettering on blue and red portions of car side; black lettering on white portions; "Built by Lionel" on side; details as found on 0864-300; third boxcar from Hobbyline dies; sprung trucks; catalogued in set 5725 in 1959 and separately 1959-61; rare with this catalogue number. **25 35 40**

0864-400 **BOSTON & MAINE** Painted light blue; unpainted black, four letterboard door; white lettering; "Built by Lionel" and full catalogue number on car side; plastic wheels; talgo-type truck; made from Hobbyline dies; catalogued 1960-61 and 1963; catalogued in set 14203 in 1963 and said to be new, although car remained unchanged from 1961. **25 35 40**

0864-700 **SANTA FE** Painted bright red; white lettering; herald and catalogue number at left of door; "Shock Control" and slogans at right of door; sprung trucks; made from Hobbyline dies; catalogued separately only 1961-62; rare. **25 35 40**

0864-900 **NEW YORK CENTRAL** Painted jade green; black and white herald at left of door; "NEW YORK" appears in red lettering in herald, and

"CENTRAL" in white lettering; "N.Y.C." appears in black lettering on a white square at right of door; catalogue number in red lettering below square; "Built by Lionel" on side; catalogued separately 1960-62.

| | 20 | 25 | 35 |

0864-925 NEW YORK CENTRAL Similar to 0864-900, except number "0864-925" appears on car instead; also, does not have "Built by Lionel" as found on earlier car; plastic trucks; 1963-type couplers; made from Hobbyline dies; catalogued in 1964 only in three freight sets, 14270, 14280 and 14300; scarce.

| | 25 | 30 | 35 |

0864-935 NEW YORK CENTRAL Similar to 0864-900; "Built by Lionel" absent; plastic trucks; 1963-type couplers; catalogued in 1963 separately and in sets 14183 and 14233.

| | 25 | 30 | 35 |

0874 NEW YORK CENTRAL New car type; new Lionel dies; low profile; light construction; painted jade green; lettering as found on other NYC cars; "0874" in red lettering at right of door; "Built by Lionel" absent; new door type with four claw feet; door rides on external guides; no number boards on door; metal frame with no detail, except truck bolster; 1963-type talgo trucks; separate black floor bracing; spartan appearance; catalogued as a separate item in 1964-65, while 0864-925 NYC appeared in sets; rare.

| | 20 | 25 | 30 |

0874-25 NEW YORK CENTRAL Identical to 0874; truck bolster on bottom; no floor bracing; "-25" added to carton only; catalogued in sets 1965-66; rare.

| | 20 | 25 | 30 |

0874-60 BOSTON & MAINE Same car type as 0874; painted medium blue; white lettering; "0874" (without suffix) on car side; "Built by Lionel" absent; catalogued 1964-65; rare.

| | 20 | 25 | 30 |

OPERATING ROLLING STOCK

0039 TRACK CLEANING CAR Unusual car type, longer than boxcars, higher cab than on steam locomotives; painted flat black plastic body; flat orange center cab; 1960-type motor drives two cleaning sponges; car unpropelled; sponges held on two vertical shafts driven by a brass worm gear; on/off switch on short end of car; white lettering; "TC-0039" and "SOUTHERN" on car side; cleaning fluid bottle, same as that used on 0 Gauge cleaning car, cradled in long end of car; buffing pad under car; car sold with two extra sponges and one wiper pad; catalogued separately in 1961-62 only; rarely found in mint condition or complete with attachments.

| | 30 | 40 | 65 |

0300 OPERATING LUMBER CAR Two-piece body; frame and operating mechanism constructed of black metal and plastic; red plastic superstructure; two stakes cast onto tilting gate; three fixed stakes hold logs, which are wooden dowels; white lettering; "T.L.C.X." and "0300"; same tripping mechanism as used with 0900 unloading ramp; ramp sold separately; log tray and logs sold with car; logs appear in various shades; catalogued in 1960 in sets 5743, 5749 and 5771, and separately 1960-63; very common.

| | 15 | 20 | 35 |

0301 OPERATING COAL CAR Black frame and mechanism as found on 0300; light gray unpainted superstructure; black lettering; keystone herald, "0301" and "PENNSYLVANIA" on side; sold with brown unloading bin and clear plastic bag of coal; catalogued in 1960 in four sets, in at least one set 1961-63 and separately 1960-66; very common, but may be incomplete.

| | 15 | 20 | 35 |

0319 OPERATING HELICOPTER CAR Light blue painted 50-foot flatcar; white lettering; "SOUTHERN PACIFIC" and "0319" on car side; red plastic helicopter body; black blade and landing gear; clear nose; helicopter same as that sold on 0 Gauge 3419 car; spring wound assembly releases helicopter when car is backed over a trip fastened to the track; car derails when operated if springs wound too tightly; sprung trucks; catalogued in 1960 separately and in sets 5737, 5745 and 5747; shown in 1960 with a large gray helicopter, unlike that actually produced; catalogued in set 5753 in 1962 and illustrated more accurately; difficult to find in good condition; see also 0319-110.

| | 25 | 30 | 45 |

0319-110 OPERATING HELICOPTER CAR Similar to 0319, except solid truck frames found on this car; lettering and number as found on 0319; 1963.

| | 25 | 30 | 45 |

0333 OPERATING SATELLITE LAUNCHING CAR Blue 50-foot flatcar; white lettering; "SOUTHERN PACIFIC" and catalogue number appear on car side; gray plastic control panel and yellow radar screen at one end; black plastic satellite at other end; chrome top on satellite; both satellite wings trimmed with white checkerboard on top; same screen and satellite also used on 0 Gauge 3519 car; catalogued in 1961 separately and in sets 5754 and 5748; catalogued separately 1962-66; very rare complete.

| (A) Sprung trucks; 1961-62. | 30 | 40 | 65 |
| (B) Solid truck frames; 1963-66. | 30 | 40 | 65 |

0337 OPERATING GIRAFFE CAR Modified 40-foot stock car body; unpainted white plastic; sliding doors; red lettering; "LIONEL LINES" and "CIRCUS CAR" on letter boards at left of door; "0337" on car body at right; long yellow shaft with giraffe head on top fastened to metal floor; metal shoe with magnet suspended from floor; when car passes beneath tell-tale, giraffe ducks its head into car; catalogued in 1961 separately, in set 5751 and in the "Valise Pack" 5767.

| (A) Poorly-matched painted white doors; common variation. | 15 | 20 | 60 |
| (B) Unpainted white plastic doors; scarce. | | | **NRS** |

0349 OPERATING TURBO MISSILE CAR 40-foot flatcar body; no lettering; unpainted blue catapult and reserve housing, each holding one missile, same as those used on 0 Gauge missile car; unpainted white plastic missiles with red center, also the same as found on 0 Gauge cars; catapult loaded by inserting missile and turning same to lock in place; fired manually; black undercarriage marked "LIONEL"; difficult to find with missiles unbroken; catalogued in 1962 separately and in sets 14043 and 14098; catalogued only separately 1963-66.

| (A) Unpainted red flatcar body. | 30 | 40 | 50 |
| (B) Maroon flatcar body; rare. | 30 | 40 | 50 |

0357 COP & HOBO CAR House-type car, similar in construction to the Railway Express refrigerator; non-opening door; unpainted light blue plastic; white lettering; "LIONEL LINES" and "0357" at left of door; "HYDRAULIC PLATFORM MAINTENANCE CAR" at right; gray plastic platform on rooftop; cop and hobo figures are transferred from the top of the car to the black plastic trestle bridge each time the car passes under the bridge; catalogued 1962-66; incorrectly illustrated with a stock car body every year except 1966; usually found without bridge or figures.

| | 20 | 25 | 90 |

0365 MINUTEMAN LAUNCHING CAR Unpainted white plastic modified Hobbyline boxcar body; separate, unpainted blue roof with two arms that secure the roof and allow it to move when the launching mechanism is tripped; blue and red; "STRATEGIC AIR COMMAND" and Air Force insignia at left of door; "U.S. AIR FORCE MINUTEMEN" and red "0365" at right; spring-loaded mechanism with four metal geared wheels and metal frame; unpainted white plastic rocket, approximately 3-1/2" long, with blue rubber tip; no fins or lettering on rocket; catalogued in 1962 separately and in sets 14033, 14064 and 14098; catalogued in 1963 separately and in set 14193; offered only separately 1964-66; rare.

| | 30 | 40 | 50 |

The 0366 Milk Car features an ingenious mechanism to deliver cans, which are inserted in a device that resembles a cap gun bullet chamber.

0366 OPERATING MILK CAR White refrigerator car; black lettering; "AUTOMATIC MILK CAR" and "0366" at left; "REFRIGERATOR LINE" and dimensional data at right; the eight metal milk cans are loaded through a door located at the center of the roof; cans are pushed through spring-loaded plug doors onto plastic loading dock; white rubber man inside; catalogued 1961-66; rarely found complete.

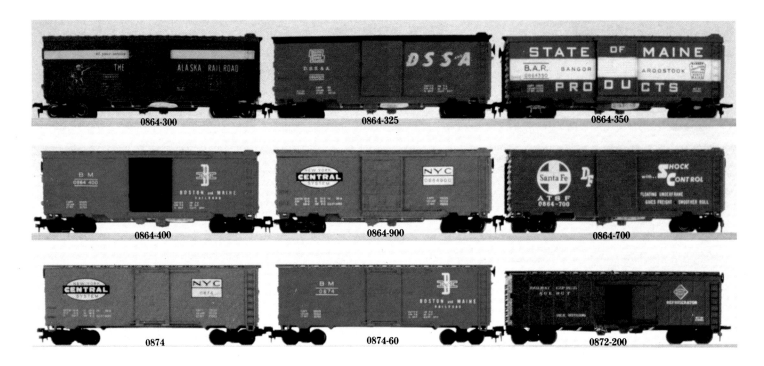

0864-300	0864-325	0864-350
0864-400	0864-900	0864-700
0874	0874-60	0872-200

Eight Lionel boxcars and the very rare Railway Express Refrigerator car (bottom right). G. Horan Collection.

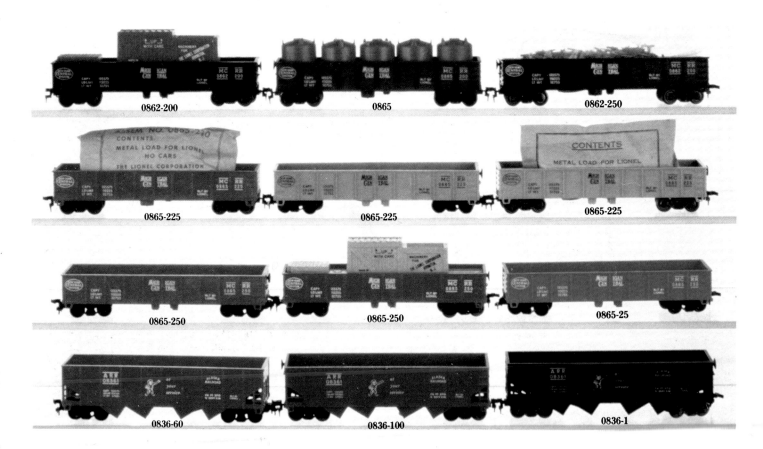

0862-200	0865	0862-250
0865-225	0865-225	0865-225
0865-250	0865-250	0865-25
0836-60	0836-100	0836-1

Open-top cars add visual interest both to children's train sets and to collectors' displays. Lionel's gondolas have a variety of loads, such as crates, cannisters and scrap metal, all shown in the cars on the top shelf. The cars at either end of the second shelf carry loads that have been carefully preserved in their original packaging. In both the gondola and hopper car series, the numbers on car sides do not correspond faithfully to catalogue numbers. Thus, the collector should read these sections with care to properly identify the pieces he has found.

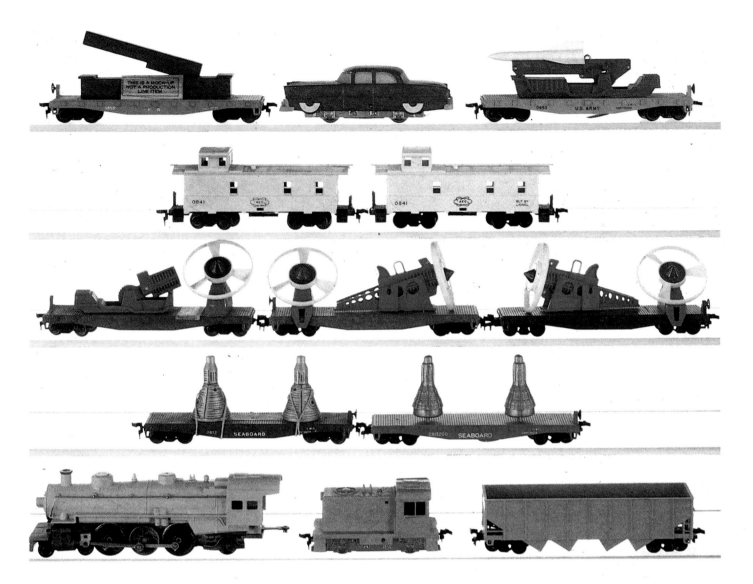

A selection of Lionel prototypes and mock-ups. The missile launcher mock-up and production items are shown on the top shelf (left and right). At top center is an inspection car prototype. The AEC caboose mock-up and production items are shown on the second shelf (left and right). A prototype satellite car (left), a production car (center) and a preproduction sample in maroon (right) appear on the third shelf. A mock-up of the Mercury capsule car with wooden capsules appears on the fourth shelf (left) next to a regular production piece. On the bottom shelf are unpainted samples of the Pacific, Husky and a hopper car.

(A) Painted body; sprung trucks; 1961-62. 15 20 50
(B) Unpainted body; solid frame trucks; 1963-66. 15 20 40

0370 OPERATING SHERIFF AND OUTLAW CAR Unpainted red plastic stock car body; yellow lettering; "Wells Fargo" and "Western Atlantic Fast Express" on two letterboards at left of door; "0370" near roof line at right; catalogued in 1962 in set 14084 and separately 1962-66.

(A) Operating version; two square holes diagonally opposed at opposite ends of roof; geared mechanism, plastic with metal arms, raise Sheriff then Outlaw so that they can exchange fire; both figures painted, Sheriff yellow and Outlaw blue; metal floor; sprung trucks; 1962. 15 20 45
(B) Similar to (A), except solid frame trucks; 1963-66. 15 20 45
(C) Non-operating version made for special Sears train sets in the early 1960s; no holes in roof; no figures nor mechanism; metal floor; solid frame trucks; rare. **NRS**

0805 A.E.C. FLATCAR Painted red 40-foot car; white lettering; "Seaboard", "0805" and "Built by Lionel" appear on car side; light gray cannister mounted on black base; power feed same as that on 0834 Poultry Car; "DANGER RADIOACTIVE WASTE" in red lettering on cannister; blinking red light under cannister; plastic truck frames; metal wheels; electrical collector-type trucks; catalogued every year 1959-66 in sets and/or separately.

(A) Early couplers without manual uncoupling pin; 1959-62. 8 10 25
(B) 1963-type couplers with manual uncoupling pin; partial copper wheel for blinker; stake holes along each side; no lettering on cannister; 1963-66; J. Otterbein and J. Kimenhour comments. 8 10 20
(C) Similar to (B); partial steel wheel for blinker; two stake holes at center of car. 8 10 20

0834 POULTRY CAR Red 40-foot modified stock car body; white lettering; "Poultry Dispatch" at left; "0834" and "Built by Lionel" at right of door; open side panels with plastic inserts; chickens painted on side panels; illuminated; chickens appear to fly when car moves; detailed underframe; sprung trucks with current collection; catalogued in 1959 in sets 5717, 5725 and 5733, and separately 1959-60.

(A) Painted car body and door; black door painted gray; 1959; T. Shepler Collection; rare. **NRS**
(B) Unpainted car body; black door painted gray; 1960 25 30 40

0847 EXPLODING TARGET RANGE CAR Four-piece body assembly; floor and ends molded together; separate roof; two separate sides; red unpainted plastic body; white lettering; round "DANGER" sign and "0847" at one side of door; "EXPLOSIVES" on other side; internal spring mechanism set like an old mousetrap — making reassembly of car very tricky; car "exploded" when struck by missile or other object; locking

51

The mechanism of the 0370 Sheriff and Outlaw Car raises and lowers each figure, so that they can exchange fire.

mechanism built into floor can be set so that car will not fly apart when used as a piece of non-operating rolling stock; sprung trucks; catalogued separately and in sets 1960-62; very common; see also 0847-100.

	12	15	20

0847-100 EXPLODING TARGET RANGE CAR Similar to 0847, except solid frame trucks are present on this car; otherwise identical to 0847; "-100" suffix appears on carton only; catalogued 1963-65. 12 15 20

0850 MISSILE LAUNCHING FLATCAR Light gray unpainted 40-foot flatcar; unpainted red firing platform; black lettering; "U.S. ARMY" and "0850" appear on side; platform pivots about single rivet fastened through car body; firing portion of platform is spring loaded and rises two inches in height; two red plastic firing arms extend from sides; rockets same as that loaded on 0823 flatcar; separate brakewheel; catalogued in sets 1960-63 and separately 1960-65; red actuator arms are often broken; see also 0850-110.
(A) Sprung trucks; 1960-62. 20 30 35
(B) Solid frame trucks; 1963-65. 20 30 35

0850-110 MISSILE LAUNCHING FLATCAR Identical to 0850(B); "110" appears on carton only; 1966. 20 30 35

0880 OPERATING MAINTENANCE CAR WITH LIGHT Painted, black 40-foot flatcar; gray and yellow work platform as found on 0870; searchlight located in place of 0870's generator; white lettering; "PENN-SYLVANIA", "Built by Lionel" and "0880" appear on car side; metal searchlight as found on the 0 Gauge four-light tower and 410 Blinking Billboard; unlike 0 Gauge car, does not have on/off switch; light remains on as long as track is powered; catalogued 1959-61 separately and in sets. 25 30 45

FLATCARS, CRANES AND MISCELLANEOUS CARS

0800-200 FLAT WITH AIRPLANE Painted flat black body; white lettering; "Seaboard Railroad", "0800-200" and "Built by Lionel" appear on car side; one-piece black plastic loading frame; same as that used on 1958 Athearn cars; separate brakewheel; sprung trucks; catalogued separately in 1960 only, but available as an uncatalogued item until 1963; difficult to find with unbroken airplane; however, airplane still offered by Athearn.
(A) Airplane with unpainted black underbody; dull orange, painted top portion, tail and wings. 15 25 40
(B) Airplane with unpainted black underbody; silver, painted top portion, tail and wings. 15 25 40

0801-200 FLAT WITH BOAT Painted flat black 40-foot body; white lettering; "Seaboard", "0801-200" and "Built by Lionel" appear on car side; separate brakewheel; made from Hobbyline dies; catalogued separate-

ly in 1960 only, but available as an uncatalogued item until 1962; boats still offered by Athearn.
(A) Boat with red hull and white top. 15 20 45
(B) Boat with blue hull and white top. 15 20 45

0806 FLATCAR WITH HELICOPTER Painted flat black 50-foot body; white lettering; "SOUTHERN PACIFIC", "0806" and "Built by Lionel" on side; separate brakewheel; sprung metal trucks; gray helicopter has single twin blade with turbo charger at each end; helicopter has gray tail; no frame or platform on car; helicopter secured with one black rubber band across its black landing gear; helicopter will operate also on an 0 Gauge launching car; many of these cannabilized by 0 Gauge collectors seeking helicopter parts; catalogued in 1959 separately and in sets 5717, 5719 and 5731; incorrectly illustrated in 1959 as a tuscan car loaded with a helicopter with double turbo blades; this helicopter was produced only in the 0 Gauge line; catalogued separately also in 1960 and shown again incorrectly as a blue flatcar.
(A) Helicopter lettered "U.S. Navy" in black. 25 30 45
(B) Unmarked helicopter. 25 30 45

0807 FLATCAR WITH BULLDOZER Painted red 40-foot car; white lettering; "N.Y.C.", "0807", "Built by Lionel" and a NYC herald appear on car side; separate brakewheel; sprung trucks; Caterpillar Bulldozer made by Lesney; the bulldozer is Number 8 in the Matchbox series; it has a yellow body, green rubber treads and gray wheels; a driver is cast onto the seat; secured to the car by a red rubber band, the bulldozer came packaged in a Matchbox carton; flatcar is weighted and marked "LIONEL" on frame; catalogued 1959 in set 5727 and separately 1959-60; illustration incorrectly shows catalogue number in the center of car and tractor with black treads; number is actually between the third and fourth stake pockets; very rare in mint-and-boxed condition. 30 35 125

0807 NYC Flatcar with Matchbox bulldozer.

0808 FLATCAR WITH TRACTOR Painted red 40-foot car; white lettering; "N.Y.C.", "0808", "Built by Lionel" and NYC herald appear on car side; separate brakewheel; sprung trucks; Red Farm Tractor made by Lesney; the tractor is Number 4 in the Matchbox series; it has a red body and gray wheels; the large wheels have painted gold centers; secured to the car by a red rubber band, the tractor came packaged in a Matchbox carton; flatcar is weighted and marked "LIONEL" on frame; catalogued in 1959 in set 5723 and separately 1959-60; incorrectly illustrated with catalogue number at center of car; very rare in mint-and-boxed condition. 30 35 125

0808 NYC Flatcar with Matchbox tractor.

0809 HELIUM TANK TRANSPORT Unpainted black 40-foot car body as used on 0861 log car; hopper car undercarriage; three wooden cylinders painted silver held in place with two black rubber bands; no lettering nor numbers on car side, although catalogue depicts a number board at car center; "LIONEL" appears on car frame; catalogued in 1961 separately and in sets 5753 and 5754; catalogued in 1962 separately and in set 14033; common. 20 25 40

0810 EMERGENCY GENERATOR TRANSPORT Black, painted 50-foot flatcar; white lettering; "SOUTHERN PACIFIC", "0810" and "Built by Lionel" appear on car side; unpainted orange generator as found on the 0 Gauge 3520 Searchlight Car; metal sprung trucks; weighted; underframe marked "LIONEL"; catalogued in 1961 in set 5762, in 1963 in set 14183 and separately 1961-63.   30   45   90

0813 MERCURY CAPSULE CAR Unpainted light blue, 40-foot flatcar; white lettering; "Seaboard" and "0813-200" appear on car side; two silver plastic capsules, the same as that used in the rocket on the 0 Gauge 3413 Capsule Launching car; two 3/4" vertical tabs cast into the floor hold the two capsules; two gray rubber bands secure the capsules to the tabs; capsules are very fragile and difficult to find; solid frame trucks; catalogued in set 14038 in 1962 and separately 1962-66; a preproduction prototype with wooden capsules is shown in the photo section; this car is the most difficult to find with its load present and in good condition.   40   50   90

0814-200 AUTO TRANSPORT Painted flat red 50-foot flatcar body; painted flat black superstructure; white lettering; "SOUTHERN PACIFIC", "0814-200" and "Built by Lionel" appear on car side; "Evans Auto Loader" on superstructure, which snaps into floor of the car and holds four plastic automobiles; automobile colors varied through the years; catalogued in 1960 only as a separate item, but available through 1962.   25   30   45

0821 PIPE CAR Unpainted black, 40-foot hopper car undercarriage as used on the Log and Helium Cars; three plastic pipes; no lettering nor numbers on car; plastic pipes; catalogued in 1960 separately and in set 5737; see also 0821-50 and 0821-100.
(A) Sprung trucks; silver pipes.   12   15   25
(B) Sprung trucks; gray pipes; T. Shepler Collection.   12   15   25
(C) Rigid-frame trucks; finger tab couplers; gray pipes; came in set 14084 in 1962; J. Otterbein and J. Kimenhour comments.   12   15   25

0821-50 PIPE CAR Yellow pipe load; otherwise identical to 0821-100; "-50" appears only on carton; catalogued in 1964 in set 14240; also catalogued 1965-66, the only years the yellow load was illustrated.
                                                         12   15   25

0821-100 PIPE CAR Solid frame plastic trucks; otherwise identical to 0821; "-100" appears only on carton; catalogued in 1963 only in set 14193.
                                                         12   15   25

0823 TWIN MISSILE TRANSPORT Red unpainted 50-foot flatcar; white lettering; "SOUTHERN PACIFIC" and "0823" on car side; two white missiles, like those on the 0 Gauge 45 Missile Launcher, mounted on black plastic frame; frame pressed into eight 1/4" slots in car floor; two thin wire straps secure missiles to black frames; weighted car; sprung metal trucks; catalogued in 1960, separately and in set 5739, and in 1961, separately and in set 5758; often incomplete.   20   30   35

0824-200 FLATCAR WITH TWO AUTOS Painted black 40-foot car; white lettering; "N.Y.C.", "0824-200" and "Built by Lionel" on car side; separate brakewheels; two automobiles, like those on the 0814 Auto Loader, secured by rubber bands; no loading frame; automobile colors varied over the production period; catalogued separately in 1960 and available through 1961.   15   20   25

0842 CULVERT PIPE CAR 40-foot tank car frame with diamond markers and vertical brakewheel; white lettering; "T.L.C.X." on one end, "0842" at other; three metal culvert pipes, like those used on 0 Gauge cars; each pipe secured by an individual black rubber band; "LIONEL" on underframe; catalogued in 1960, separately in 1960 and available through 1961.
(A) Sprung metal trucks; 1960.   20   25   30
(B) Solid metal truck side frames; plastic wheels; 1961. 20   25   30

0845 GOLD TRANSPORT CAR Clear plastic refrigerator car body; painted silver; portions of sides masked from paint and thus left clear to reveal gold bricks which are cast into the floor; black lettering; "0845" next to door; "FORT KNOX GOLD RESERVE" under windows; door modeled to represent bank vault door; 0357 car also has this type of door; weighted floor; "LIONEL" on underframe; solid frame Talgo trucks; catalogued in 1962 in set 14084 and separately 1962-66; rare.   40   50   95

0860 DERRICK CAR Painted semi-gloss gray; black lettering; "PENN-SYLVANIA", "0860-200" and "Built by Lionel" appear on car side; unpainted black plastic derrick with fine brass chain; two toolboxes and

sidewalls painted gray; fragile derrick breaks easily; catalogued in 1960, separately and in sets, and separately 1961-63; rare.
(A) Sprung trucks; 1960-62.   20   30   45
(B) Solid frame trucks; 1963.   20   30   45

0861 LOG CAR Unpainted black 40-foot hopper car frame; no lettering nor numbers on car; three darkly colored logs secured by two black rubber bands; approximately 3/8" in diameter, logs have a coat of glue and sawdust to simulate bark texture; sprung metal trucks; "LIONEL" on underframe; catalogued separately and in sets 1959-62; see also 0861-110.
                                                         15   20   25

0861-110 LOG CAR Solid frame trucks; lightly colored logs; otherwise identical to 0861; catalogued 1963-66 separately and in various sets.
                                                         15   20   25

0863 FLATCAR WITH RAIL TRUCKS Unpainted red 50-foot car; white lettering; "SOUTHERN PACIFIC" and "0863" are the only markings; three 1959-type freight car trucks mounted on unpainted black plastic frame like that used on the 0823 Missile Car; loading frame presses into holes in the car floor; separate brakewheel; weighted underframe; sprung trucks; "LIONEL" on underframe; catalogued in 1960, separately and in set 5749, and in 1961 in set 5762; the 1962 catalogue incorrectly illustrates this car with the Pennsylvania road name, which is spelled incorrectly to boot!
                                                         20   25   30

0866-200 CIRCUS CAR Unpainted white plastic 40-foot stock car; painted white operating doors; flat red roofwalk; red lettering; "LIONEL LINES" and "CIRCUS CAR" on letterboards at left of door; "0866-200" and "Built by Lionel" at right; sprung trucks; detailed underframe with weight; very similar to 0 Gauge version; catalogued in set 5721 in 1959 and separately 1959-60; rare.   15   20   35

0870 MAINTENANCE FLATCAR WITH GENERATOR Painted, red body; white lettering; "PENNSYLVANIA", "0870" and "Built by Lionel" appear on car side; gray, painted platform at one end; gray generator housing at other end; movable yellow work platform with fragile railings, as found on 0880 Maintenance Car; catalogued in set 5723 in 1959 and separately 1959-60.   30   35   40

0872-200 RAILWAY EXPRESS REFRIGERATOR Painted, deep green body; red Railway Express decal herald at right of door; gold lettering; "Built by Lionel" and "0872-200" appear on car side; three heavy steps on each side; black plastic opening doors; produced from Lionel tooling; catalogued 1959-61; extremely rare.   20   30   70

0873 RODEO CAR Unpainted yellow 40-foot car body as used of 0370 with non-operating doors; two holes in each side of car; red lettering; "Horse Transport Car" at left of door; "Fast Express" and "0873" at right; no number boards; vertical shaft at center of car floor holds plastic arm, which extends the length of the car; a double horse head casting is fastened to each end of the arm; the arm moves from side to side when the car rolls, thus the horses appear to sway in and out the window; detailed underframe; solid frame trucks; catalogued separately and in sets 1962-66.
(A) One brown horse head and one white horse head on either side.
                                                         15   20   30
(B) Two brown horse heads on each side; J. Otterbein and J. Kimenhour comments.   15   20   30

0875 FLATCAR WITH MISSILE Painted black 40-foot car; white lettering; "Seaboard", "0875" and "Built by Lionel" appear on car side; plastic missile with rubber tip, as found on 0 Gauge 6650 Flatcar; "LIONEL" appears on weighted underframe; catalogued in 1959 separately and in sets 5719 and 5725; the catalogue illustration incorrectly shows that car with a brown or tuscan body; catalogued in 1960, separately and in set 5747, and in 1961, in set 5752.
(A) Red and white rocket; blue rubber tip; 1959-61.   15   20   25
(B) White rocket; blue rubber tip; not shown in catalogue illustration; 1961 only.   15   20   25

0889 ILLINOIS CENTRAL CRANE CAR Unpainted black plastic frame, boom and top access door; two metal hooks; one-piece housing and pulley assembly; components (non-operating) attached to boom with metal pin; boom and access door raised and lowered by two wires; two metal cranks provided with car, but they do not operate the boom; flat orange cab with dark green lettering; "ILLINOIS CENTRAL" at rear of cab; "N.W.W.

0838	0837-100	0837
0827-50	0827-75	0827(B)
0827(A)	0817-350	0817-325
0817-275	0817-150	0840
0840	0841	0841-125
0841-50	0841-85	0841-175

Cabooses manufactured by Lionel Corporation are obviated by the body-mounting tabs found on the car side, just above the toolbox on the side shown. The amount of detail on any given caboose depended upon Lionel's price target. As evidenced by the cabooses in this illustration, which have been preserved as they were purchased, the cars were sold with or without end ladders, brakewheels and smokestacks, in many combinations.

200" just ahead of cab door; "0889" on rear cab skirting; cab held to boom frame with three tabs that pass through the cab, one on either side and a third at the rear; cab and thin metal weight held to car frame with pressure nut; blackened six-wheel trucks, screw-mounted to frame; "LIONEL" on truck frames; catalogued in 1961 separately and in set 5762; catalogue incorrectly shows a red crane; also catalogued in 1962, separately and in sets, and in 1963, separately and in sets 14193 and 14233. **30   50   80**

TANK CARS

0815-50 ROCKET FUEL Unpainted black frame; flat white, painted tank body; red lettering; "0815" appears above the wire handrails; no red lines around catalogue number, as found on 0816; "-50" suffix does not appear on car; "Rocket Fuel", "Liquified Hydrogen" and "Danger" appear below

the handrails; black plastic platform around single dome; metal ladder extends from platform to frame on each side and secures tank body to frame; "Made by Lionel", "N.Y.N.Y." and "USA" appear on underframe; solid frame trucks; separate brakewheel; catalogued in 1963, in sets 14143 and 14230, and in 1964, in set 14300; the illustration of set 14300 incorrectly shows the orange Lionel Lines tank car; catalogued in 1966 in set 14300.

15   25   35

0815-75 LIONEL LINES Unpainted black frame; flat orange, painted body; black band under platform; body secured to frame with metal ladders from platform; black lettering; "LIONEL LINES", "0815-200" and the Lionel logo appear on car side; separate brakewheel; catalogued in 1963 in sets 14153, 14183 and 14233; the "-75" appears in the illustrations, but not on the actual car; catalogued in set 14300 in 1965-66, but listed with the Rocket Fuel tank car number; difficult to find with unbroken platform; see also 0815-85. **20   25   35**

Athearn Pacific   Athearn 0814(A)

Athearn 0865(A)   Athearn 0864-175   Athearn 0836(A)

Athearn 0879(A)   Athearn 0819-100

0625LT   0805

0834   0806   0872-200

0800   0817

Two Lionel train sets. The top set was assembled with an Athearn Pacific locomotive made in 1960 to show what this set would have looked like if Athearn had been able to supply the projected Hi-F powered Pacific it had offered for 1958. This train was never actually offered as a set by Lionel. The second set illustrates a legitimate Lionel set, produced with the 0625 Pacific.

0815-85 LIONEL LINES Unpainted black frame; no wire handrails nor ladders; dull unpainted orange body; thin black lettering; "LIONEL LINES", "0815-200" and Lionel logo appear on car side; red triangular placards on frame; solid truck frames; finger tab couplers; catalogued separately in 1963 only; see also 0815-75.

(A) With platform; T. Shepler Collection.	20	25	35
(B) Without platforms.	20	25	35

0815-110 SUN OIL CO. Unpainted black frame; body secured to frame with metal ladders from platform; wire handrails present; semi-gloss black, painted body; white lettering; "SUNOCO" and "N.A.T.X. 25064" appear on car side; no Lionel number; separate brakewheel; "LIONEL", "N.Y.N.Y." and "USA" appear on car frame; solid frame trucks; uncatalogued; this car came in set 14310 in place of a Rocket Fuel tank listed and illustrated on the set box; car in sealed set held in Collection of Vincent Rosa; very rare.   25   30   125

0815-200 LIONEL LINES See 0815-75 and 0815-85 for description.

0816 ROCKET FUEL Unpainted black plastic frame; flat white, painted frame; red lettering; "0816", with red border, above handrails; "Rocket Fuel", "Liquified Hydrogen" and "Danger" below handrails; red outline of rocket; sprung trucks; catalogued separately in 1962; see also 0816-50.

     10   15   35

0816-50 ROCKET FUEL Solid frame trucks; otherwise identical to 0816; "-50" does not appear on car side; catalogued separately 1963-66.

     10   15   35

HOPPER CARS

0836-1 ALASKA QUAD HOPPER Painted flat black; orange lettering "Alaska Railroad", "08361", "Built by Lionel" and the Alaskan boy appear on car side; made from Hobbyline dies; catalogued in 1959 separately and In set 5725; the car is shown incorrectly in both blue and yellow and black and white schemes; catalogued again in 1960 in set 5749 and separately 1960-63; see also 0836-60 and 0836-100.   15   20   35

0836-60 ALASKA QUAD HOPPER Red body; "ALASKA RAILROAD", white lettering; "08631", "Built by Lionel" and the Alaskan boy appear on car side; solid frame plastic trucks; catalogued in 1961 in set 5755; available

as an uncatalogued item 1962-64: catalogued separately and in sets 1965-66; see also 0836 and 0836-100.
(A) Painted red body; scarce.   **NRS**
(B) Unpainted red body.   **10   15   25**

0836-100   ALASKA QUAD HOPPER Solid truck frames and 1963-type couplers; catalogued in 1963.
(A) Painted flat black; orange lettering; similar to 0836. **10   20   35**
(B) Unpainted red body; white lettering; similar to 0836-60(B).
                                                     10   15   25

GONDOLA CARS

The Lionel Corporation gondolas are among the most difficult to sort of Lionel H0 models. The brown 0865 made in 1959 was the first and most attractive of these gondolas. In the following years, Lionel worked to produce models at lower and lower costs. Thus, by 1963, there were no longer loads in any of the gondolas, and all of these cars were simply molded in appropriate colors, as none were painted. After 1963 the catalogue number and/or the suffix changed almost every year, although the car itself remained unchanged. For example, the blue 0865-400 of 1964 was catalogued and packaged with the suffix -425 in 1964 and -435 in 1965 and 1966. However, the car carried the number 0865-250 throughout this period. The red 0865-225 received similar treatment. The listing of gondolas is presented as clearly as possible. Cross-references are provided to assist the collector in the identification of these cars.

0862   See 0862-200 and 0862-250.

0862-200   GONDOLA WITH RED CRATES Uncatalogued, 1960-61; similar to 0862-250; black car; see also 0862-250.
(A) Loaded with red plastic wooden crates; "MACHINERY FOR THE LIONEL CORPORATION IRVINGTON, N.J." in white lettering on crates; these crates were also available at the same time in a three-car set headed by the 0058 Rock Island Husky; this set was catalogued by Kutler's Toy Store in the Germantown section of Philadelphia, Pa.
                                            Verification Requested
(B) Loaded with scrap metal; T. Shepler Collection.   **NRS**

0862-250   GONDOLA WITH SCRAP METAL Flat black, painted body; white lettering; "Michigan Central", "MCRR", "0862-200" and NYC System herald appear on car side; "Built by Lionel" also present; sold with a bag of scrap metal slugs as provided for 0 Gauge operating cranes; load much too heavy for the smaller cars; catalogued in 1959 separately and in set 5729; "0862-250" appears on carton; only 0862 portion of number used in catalogue; difficult to find with original slugs. **10   15   20**

0865   GONDOLA WITH CANNISTERS Painted, dark flat brown body; yellowish-gold lettering; NYC System herald at left; "Michigan Central" at center; "M.C.R.R." and "0865-200" with underscore at right; "Built by Lionel" also present; separate brakewheel; five unmarked red cannisters; sprung metal trucks; first 0865-series gondola; catalogued in 1959 separately and in set 5727; catalogue incorrectly shows the Athearn car with cannisters; scarce; see also 0865-400.   **20   25   35**

0865-225   GONDOLA WITH SCRAP METAL NYC System herald; "Michigan Central", "M.C.R.R." and "0865-225" on car side; "Built by Lionel" also present; separate brakewheel; metal slugs for load; sprung trucks.
(A) Unpainted gray plastic body; black lettering; catalogued 1960-62; illustrations incorrectly show the car as black. **10   15   20**
(B) Unpainted red plastic body; white lettering; catalogued in 1962 only in sets 14023 and 10484.   **10   15   20**

0865-250   GONDOLA WITH CRATES Flat red, painted body; white lettering; NYC System herald; "Michigan Central", "M.C.R.R." and "0865-250" on car side; unpainted tan plastic crates; sprung trucks; catalogued in 1960, in sets 5735, 5743 and 5745, in 1961, separately and in sets 5751 and 5757, and in 1962, in sets 14003 and 14007; see also 0865-375 and 0865-400.   **10   15   20**

0865-335   GONDOLA WITH SCRAP METAL Solid frame trucks; otherwise identical to 0865-225, including number on car side; catalogued in 1963.   **10   15   20**

0865-375   GONDOLA Solid frame trucks; no crates; otherwise identical to 0865-250, including number on car side; catalogued in 1963-64.
                                                     10   15   20

0865-400   GONDOLA Unpainted blue plastic body; white Michigan Central lettering; "0865-250" and "Built by Lionel" on car side; no load; no brakewheel; solid frame trucks. The plainest of the gondolas, this car has a confusing catalogue history. In 1964, it was catalogued as 0865-400 in sets and as separately 0865-435; in 1965-66, it was catalogued with the 1959 catalogue number of 0865 without a suffix. Note, however, that all of these cars carry the number 0865-250 on the car side.   **6   10   15**

0865-425   GONDOLA   See 0865-400.

0865-435   GONDOLA   See 0865-400.

CABOOSE SHELLS AND FRAMES

All of the Lionel cabooses follow the Santa Fe offset-cupola steel caboose design. The body shell is a one-piece casting, with the roofwalk molded in place and a tab at each end to secure the body to the frame. Few of the cabooses released after 1963 came with any separate detail parts. The frame changed only slightly through the period. It is a one-piece black plastic casting with steps, toolbox, coupler pockets, valves and floor bracing molded in place. All frames are marked "LIONEL" and "N.Y.N.Y." The frame also has a tab on each side for interlocking the body and frame. A few of the cars are illuminated; these have special trucks for electrical collection as used on the operating cars. It appears that the catalogue number 0817 covers the years 1959-1960, while 0827 covers 1961-1963. Several additional numbers 0838, 0840, 0841 and 0873, represent production from 1961-1966. The variety of road names, many of which were produced for only a year or two, presents an interesting challenge for the collector. The early and late frame types may be distinguished as follows. Note that 1962 cabooses may be found with either frame type.

Frame Types

1. Early frame, 1960-1961; part number molded on bottom; generally found with sprung trucks.
2. Later frame, 1963-1966; no part number; found with solid frame trucks.

0817-150   A.T.S.F. Flat red, painted body; white lettering; only "0817" and "A.T.S.F." on car side; "Built by Lionel" absent; Type 1 frame with sprung trucks; catalogued in 1960, separately and in sets 5745, 5747 and 5771, and in 1961, separately and in set 5758.   **10   15   35**

0817-275   NEW HAVEN Flat black, painted body; white lettering; "-275" does not appear on car side; decorated like 1959 Athearn caboose, which has the same stock number; Type 2 frame with solid frame trucks; no ladders nor railings; catalogued in 1963 separately and in set 14153. **15   20   35**

0817-325   UNION PACIFIC Painted flat yellow body; flat gray cupola; bright red lettering; "UNION PACIFIC" and "0817" on car side; "Built by Lionel" absent; two separate brakewheels; separate wire handrails and metal ladders; Type 1 frame with part number; metal sprung trucks; uncatalogued; only sold separately in 1960-61.   **10   15   35**

0817-350   ROCK ISLAND White lettering; "Rock Island", "0817" and herald appear on car side; "Built by Lionel" absent; separate wire handrails and metal ladders; Type 1 frame; sprung metal trucks; catalogued in 1960 only in set 5735.
(A) Painted flat black body.   **15   20   35**
(B) Red body; black cupola; J. Otterbein and J. Kimenhour comments.
                                                                NRS

0827 SAFETY FIRST ILLUMINATED Painted flat red body; white lettering; "SAFETY FIRST" and "0827" on car side; catalogued in 1961, separately and in set 5757, and separately 1962-63; illustrations in the later catalogues incorrectly show the car with M.St.L. markings.

(A) Illuminated; separate smokestack; two separate brakewheels; wire handrails and metal ladders; Type 1 frame; collector trucks; frosted window shell insert.   **25   30   70**

(B) Unlighted; no separate details; believed to have been made as an uncatalogued item in 1964.   **Verification Requested**

0827-50 A.E.C. Unpainted white plastic body; red lettering as found on 0817-200 Athearn caboose of 1959, except number differs; separate smokestack; two separate brakewheels; Type 2 frame; solid frame trucks; catalogued in 1963 in set 14183; catalogue incorrectly describes car as illuminated; rare.   **15   20   30**

(A) "0841" on car side; no handrails; no ladders.   **15   20   30**

(B) "0827" on car side; handrails and ladders present; frosted window inserts; T. Shepler Collection.   **15   20   30**

0827-75 A.T.S.F. ILLUMINATED Flat red, painted body; white lettering; "A.T.S.F." and "0827" appear on car side; separate smokestack; two separate brakewheels; wire handrails and metal ladders; Type 2 frame; solid frame collector trucks; catalogued in 1963 only, in set 14203; scarce.

(A) Clear window insert.   **20   25   35**

(B) Frosted window insert.   **20   25   35**

0837 M.ST.L. Painted red body; white lettering; "M.ST.L." and "0837" on car side; "Built by Lionel" absent; separate smokestack; two separate brakewheels; no handrails nor ladders.

(A) Type 1 frame; sprung metal trucks; catalogued in 1961, in set 5750, and in 1962, in set 14003.   **10   15   20**

(B) Type 2 frame; solid frame trucks; identical to 0837-100; catalogued in 1964-66.   **10   15   20**

0837-100 M.ST.L. Same as original 0837(A), except solid frame trucks and Type 2 frame; in 1964, the suffix disappeared and the caboose became 0837 again; see 0837(B); catalogued 1963.   **10   15   20**

0838 ERIE Light gray, painted body; red lettering; only "0838" and diamond-shaped "E" herald appear on car side; "Built by Lionel" absent; separate smokestack; two separate brakewheels; no handrails nor ladders; Type 1 frame; sprung trucks; catalogued in 1961, in set 5751, and in 1962, in set 14013; not sold separately; scarce.   **20   25   45**

0840 N.Y.C. Painted flat black; white lettering; "N.Y.C." and "0840" on car side; "Built by Lionel" absent; separate smokestack; two separate brakewheels; no handrails nor ladders; Type 1 frame; sprung trucks; catalogued in 1961 only in set 5755; no mention of item being new; scarce.
                                                            20   25   40

0841 UNLETTERED Painted flat red; white "0841" on car side; no additional lettering; Type 1 frame; sprung trucks; catalogued in 1961, in sets 5734 and 5752, and in 1962, in five different sets; common; see also 0841-125.   **10   15   20**

0841-50 UNION PACIFIC Unpainted light yellow body; bright red lettering; "UNION PACIFIC" and "0841" appear on car side; "Built by Lionel" absent; separate smokestack; two separate brakewheels; Type 2 frame; catalogued in 1962 only in set 14033; one of the few unpainted cabooses; rare.

(A) Entire body unpainted yellow plastic.   **15   20   50**

(B) Cupola painted red; remainder of body unpainted.   **15   20   50**

0841-85 A.T.S.F. Painted flat red; white lettering; "A.T.S.F." and "0841" on car side; separate smokestack; two separate brakewheels; Type 1 frame; sprung metal trucks; catalogued in 1962 only in set 14084; scarce; see also 0841-175.   **10   15   20**

0841-125 UNLETTERED Type 2 frame; solid frame trucks; otherwise identical to 0841, including number on car side; catalogued 1963 in set 14143.   **10   15   20**

0841-175 A.T.S.F. Type 2 frame; solid frame trucks; otherwise identical to 0841-85; catalogued in 1963 only in set 14143.   **10   15   20**

0841-185 A.T.S.F. Unpainted red body; white lettering; Type 2 frame; no brakewheel; no smokestack nor handrails; "0841-185" appears on end of box; J. Otterbein and J. Kimenhour comments.   **10   15   20**

WORK CABOOSES

0819-200 BOSTON & MAINE Painted light blue; white lettering; "BM" logo on large letterboard between windows; "Built by Lionel" on the second letterboard closest to the window; "0819-200" on third letterboard at other end of cab; separate black plastic smokestack; two separate brakewheels; wire handrail and metal ladder; weighted with a metal slug; "LIONEL" appears on frame; sprung trucks with plastic bolster; two holes in the floor at the open end of car, but car has no load or derrick; catalogued in 1961 only in set 5762. This is the only work caboose for which Lionel did not offer a locomotive in a matching paint scheme. A Boston & Maine Alco was considered but not made; the Lionel prototype is illustrated in the first color plate in this chapter.   **15   20   35**

0819-225 SANTA FE Entire car painted light flat gray; red and yellow herald on side of cabin; yellow lettering; "0819-225" and "Built by Lionel" on letterboards; separate smokestack and brakewheel; wire handrail and metal ladders; sprung trucks with plastic bolsters; catalogued in 1959, separately and in set 5733, and in 1960, in sets 5737, 5741 and 5749; sold uncatalogued in 1961-62.   **15   20   35**

0819-250 NORTHERN PACIFIC Painted flat black; semi-gloss red cabin, fence and toolboxes; black and white herald on cabin side; "0819-250" appears in black letters on car side; "LIONEL" on frame and coupler pocket; one brakewheel; wire handrail and metal ladders; catalogued in 1960 only in set 5743; rare.   **15   20   35**

0819-275 CHESAPEAKE AND OHIO Painted semi-gloss dark blue; bright yellow lettering; "CO" logo on large board between windows; "0819-275" on second letterboard; separate smokestack and brakewheel; wire handrail and metal ladder; sprung metal trucks; catalogued in 1960-62 separately and in sets; see also 0819-285.   **12   15   30**

0819-285 CHESAPEAKE AND OHIO Solid frame plastic trucks; otherwise identical to 0819-275, including number on car side; catalogued in 1963, separately and in sets 14193 and 14233.   **12   15   30**

ACCESSORIES

0110 GRADUATED TRESTLE SET Unpainted gray plastic; four piers and twenty-two risers; twenty-four metal track clips; catalogued in 1958-66; common.   **5   15   20**

0111 TRESTLE SET Unpainted gray plastic; twelve "A" piers as used in the 0110 set; twenty-four metal track clips; catalogued in 1960-66; more difficult to find complete.   **3   5   20**

0114 ENGINE HOUSE WITH HORN Light gray sheet metal base with horn unit as found in 027 diesels riveted in place; heavy plastic building; walls painted red; unpainted tan corners and roof; two clear plastic windows in each side wall; four clear plastic sky lights in roof; two door openings in each end of building; building fastened to floor with two screws, which pass through roof; "LIONEL" and "0114" stamped on metal frame; requires "D" size battery; catalogued in 1958-60.   **15   25   55**

0115 ENGINE HOUSE Kit version of 0114, except no horn unit; "LIONEL" and "0115" stamped on metal floor; colors as described for 0114; catalogued in 1961-63; V. Rosa Collection; scarce.   **20   25   60**

0117 ENGINE HOUSE Assembled version of 0115, witout horn; gray, painted walls; unpainted tan corners and roof; catalogued in 1959-60; scarce.   **20   25   60**

0118 ENGINE HOUSE WITH WHISTLE Sheet metal base with plastic whistle housing, as used in 027 steam locomotive tenders, screwed in place; gray, painted walls; unpainted tan corners and roof; "LIONEL" and "0118" stamped on base; catalogued in 1958-62; some boxes contained Ray-O-Vac batteries; V. Rosa observation.   **25   30   70**

0119 TUNNEL Painted cardstock; 10" high, 12" long; painted concrete tunnel portals, extremely difficult to find, especially in good condition, but generally unwanted by collectors; catalogued in 1959-66.   **5   8   25**

0140 OPERATING BANJO SIGNAL Unpainted black plastic; lighted; 1/4" diameter metal tube connects base to upper signal housing; electrical connections concealed in base; "LIONEL" on base; vibrating mechanism which activates the swinging warning sign, which is marked "STOP", enclosed in a small metal housing—often missing; "RAILROAD CROSS-

0494   0140   0282   0197

0480   0145

Lionel prided itself on the operating accessories it offered, such as the Rotating Beacon, Banjo Signal, Crane and Radar Antenna shown on the top shelf (left to right). The crane utilized the basic body and boom from the 0899 Illinois Central Crane Car. The H0 line also included its share of military accessories, such as the Missile Firing Range shown on the lower shelf, as well as a model of the classic Automatic Gateman. The 943 Ammunition Dump shown on the lower shelf comes from the 0 Gauge line, but it is small enough to be used with the H0 firing range.

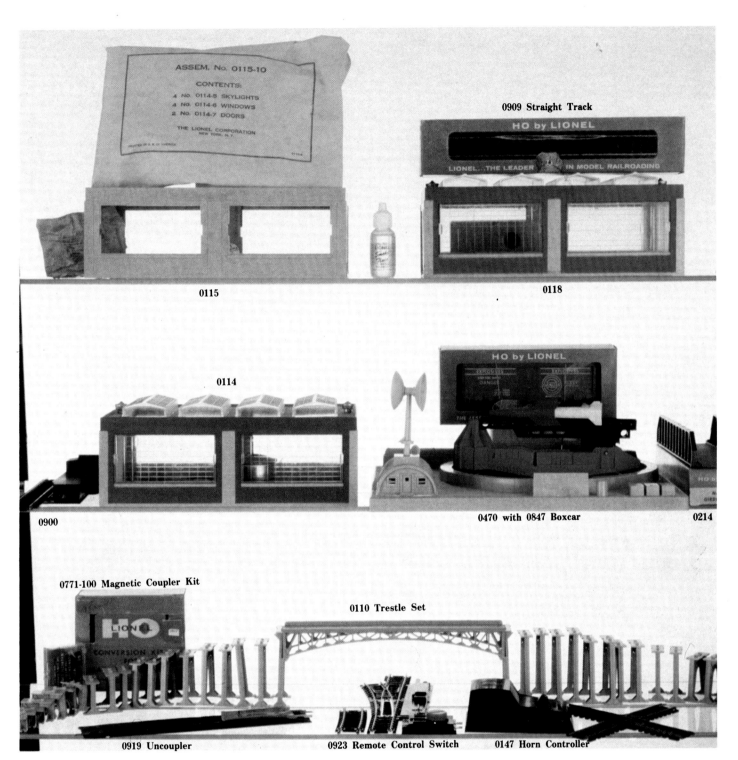

ASSEM. No. 0115-10

CONTENTS:
4 NO. 0114-5 SKYLIGHTS
4 NO. 0114-6 WINDOWS
2 NO. 0114-7 DOORS

THE LIONEL CORPORATION
NEW YORK, N.Y.

0909 Straight Track

HO by LIONEL

LIONEL...THE LEADER IN MODEL RAILROADING

0115

0118

0114

HO by LIONEL

0900

0470 with 0847 Boxcar

0214

0771-100 Magnetic Coupler Kit

0110 Trestle Set

0919 Uncoupler

0923 Remote Control Switch

0147 Horn Controller

Tucked inside the left-hand door of the first engine house on the top shelf is a package containing three smoke capsules for early H0 Pacific locomotives. The engine house on the left is a kit, whereas the one on the right came fully assembled. A plastic bottle of smoke fluid stands between the two buildings, while a box of 0909 straight track rests atop the enginehouse at right.

The Remote Control Track 0900, which is used to operate milk, coal and log cars, appears at the extreme left of the second shelf. The 0114 Engine House contains a horn, which is visible through the right-hand window. The 0470 Missile Firing Range is the largest H0 accessory, and it is the same, except for the car, as the 0 Gauge set. The 0214 Girder Bridge at the extreme right is constructed of two plastic sides riveted to a metal base.

The bottom shelf shows a variety of smaller accessory items. The

0771-100 H0 Conversion Kit for a Set of 10 Magnetic Couplers is contained in the orange box at left. The 0110 Trestle Set, shown across the shelf, consists of twenty-two risers and four "A" risers (at the right of the bridge). The track section at left is a 0919 Rerailer Uncoupler. On top of the Rerailer track is the 0428 Plastic Oil Container.

Beneath the bridge appears the 0923 Left-hand Remote Control Switch from 1962-66, complete with a green and black three-wire cable and a 0922-102 Control Button. The large controller between the switch and the track crossing is the 0147 Horn Controller for the 0535W Santa Fe B unit diesel with horn. The controller accompanied the unit each year the latter was sold. The 0990 90-degree crossing is stamped "THE LIONEL CORPORATION/NEW YORK NEW YORK." Earlier crossings were made by Atlas.

ING" boards at top; "STOP WHEN SWINGING" sign on post; packaged with instruction sheet and an operating track section; copied from the 0 Gauge line; catalogued in 1962-66.   20   25   60

0145 AUTOMATIC GATEMAN Silver plastic building; red roof, door, windows and road crossing sign; frosted plastic window inserts; small blue rubber figure with lantern; non-operating lantern molded with figure, but painted red; unpainted tan plastic base; operates with track pressure switch included in original packages; house illuminated; electrical contacts on concealed sheet metal base; "LIONEL" and "0145" stamped on metal base; copied from 0 Gauge line; catalogued in 1959-66.   20   25   40

0197 RADAR ANTENNA Plastic; 7-1/2" tall; gray, painted base; unpainted black plastic superstructure and red plastic top; two-piece silver and black radar screen with separate base, which fits over the coil mechanism that drives the screen with a rubber washer; central metal rod carries current to the driving coil mounted at its top; metal ladder serves as a ground; originally packaged with two wires, instruction sheet and black whip antenna, which fits into one corner of the upper red platform; no on/off switch included, but unit which uses a.c. may be used with 364C control button; "LIONEL" and "0197" stamped on base; always packaged in orange window box; copied from 0 Gauge line; catalogued in 1958-61.
25   30   45

0214 GIRDER BRIDGE Painted flat black; sheet metal base with plastic sides riveted in place; no lettering; "LIONEL" and "0214" stamped on metal frame and inside each side; packaged in an orange and white solid carton with a picture of the bridge on its top; 1-1/2" wide, 9" long, 1-1/4" high; common.   5   10   15

0221 TRUSS BRIDGE AND TRESTLES Unpainted gray plastic bridge; includes trestles from 0110 graduated set and 3" bridge piers; catalogued in 1961 only.   5   10   15

0222 DECK BRIDGE AND TRESTLES Unpainted gray plastic bridge; includes trestles from 0110 and 3" bridge piers; catalogued in 1961 only.
5   10   15

0224 GIRDER BRIDGE AND TRESTLES Painted black bridge (0214); includes trestles from 0110 and 3" bridge piers; catalogued in 1961 only.
5   10   15

0282 GANTRY CRANE Plastic superstructure and base from Radar Tower and Light Beacon; black plastic boom with two wire guides and two metal hooks; two plastic spools hidden inside cab, one to raise and lower the boom, the other to operate the larger hook; manually operated with two metal cranks; flat orange, painted cab with light green lettering; "Illinois Central" logo and "N.W.W. 200" on cab; catalogue number 0282 on skirting below cab floor; catalogued in 1961-63; shell is the same as that used on 0889 Crane, with number changed; rare.   35   40   100

0470 I.R.B.M. MISSILE LAUNCH PLATFORM Unpainted 11" x 12" tan plastic base, similar to a turntable pit; manually-operated blue and black rocket launcher mounted within circle; red and white rocket with blue rubber tip; Quonset hut molded into base at one corner; yellow horn and two-sided antenna dish on roof of hut; red 0847 Explosive Boxcar included in separate carton; rocket and platform same as those used on 0 Gauge Satellite Car; set packed in solid orange carton with black lettering; catalogued in 1960 and 1962; available uncatalogued in 1961; difficult to find complete set.
25   35   50

0480 MISSILE FIRING RANGE Same type of unpainted tan base as that on 470, but without round pit; two-section base; one section holds Lychen trees included with set; larger section bears gray firing platform; four white missiles; blue rubber figure; firing platform, missiles and figure identical to those on 0 Gauge 6544 Missile Car; catalogued in 1962-63; difficult to find complete.   25   40   85

0494 ROTATING BEACON 7" tall; base 3" square; unpainted black plastic tower housing; one red and one green plastic lens; red tower railing; metal ladder and center pole supply current to bulb at top and secure tower to base; brown unpainted base with four rubber pads; "LIONEL" and catalogue number on base; driven with rubber finger washer as used in 0 Gauge models; 14-16 volt a.c. operation; catalogued 1959-63; difficult to find unbroken.   20   30   45

0900 REMOTE CONTROL TRACK Used with all remote-controlled operating cars from 1960 to 1966; 9" section of track with ramp, directions for use and 0190 control button; maroon plastic housing detailed like wooden boards; black plastic bottom frame; metal arm extends towards track and trips car mechanisms; operates with a 14-16 volt a.c. power pack.
8   10   40

SCENIC ACCESSORIES

All of the buildings, trees, telephone poles and figures were made by Plasticville and sold both in the Lionel and Plasticville catalogues. The Lionel accessories were packaged in the distinctive orange and white boxes, but the parts contain no Lionel identification. Once unpacked, the accessories are indistinguishable from regular Plasticville items, although colors occasionally varied between the two lines. Only an item found in an unopened Lionel carton can be identified as a Lionel product.

First catalogued in 1959, the scenic accessories were offered through 1962. Some items appeared in only one catalogue, although most were available for at least two years. Only the figures and billboard sets were catalogued in 1963. By 1964 Lionel had discontinued the figures, and only the 0310 Billboard set remained. Each set came with an illustrated instruction sheet, and the later sets that required painting came with paints and a separate sheet with painting instructions. With the exception of coloration, the catalogue pictures are fairly accurate in showing the actual contents of each accessories package. Most of the items remain available in the current Plasticville line, although, as we noted, the colors vary.

0310 BILLBOARD SET Five dark green plastic frames; five printed color posters, each with the name of a prominent advertiser; the H0 posters do not resemble those in the 0 Gauge line; the H0 posters have a white background without the green border used on the 0 Gauge posters; the following poster names have been identified: 1959 "Join the Navy", Underwood Typewriters, Navy — Space Age, Chevrolet Used Cars and Trucks, Cities Service Eager Beaver, Airex Reels, Target Range, Join the Navy, Juicyfruit, Lionel H0, Lionel Spear, Navy "Stay in School", Big Gallon, Swifts Franks, Finish Line, Lionel Science Series and Lionel Porter; catalogued in 1959-66.   3   5   10

0410 RANCH HOUSE SET Eight-piece set; aqua blue walls; white roof and trim; two telephone poles; five pine trees with brown plastic trunks; six separate green pieces stack on each trunk; trees are scarce; catalogued in 1959; available uncatalogued in 1960-61.   5   10   12

0411 FIGURE SET Sixteen-piece set; twelve unpainted plastic figures, with paint set and brush; unpainted plastic watchman's shanty with gray walls and base, and light brown roof and trim; small jar of styrene cement with a caution for indoor use included with paint set; figures also available in other sets; difficult to find in Lionel packaging; catalogued in 1959 only.
5   8   10

0412 FARM SET Eighteen-piece set; barn, silo and Cape Cod farmhouse; all buildings have white walls, red roofs and red trim; also includes dog, two cows and thirteen chickens; all figures unpainted brown plastic; catalogued in 1959 only. **5 10 15**

0413 RAILROAD STRUCTURE SET Seven-piece set, unpainted plastic.
(A) Gray water tower with brown roof and trim; gray switch tower also with brown roof and trim; gray freight shed with brown roof and ends; four brown telephone poles; catalogued in 1959. **5 10 15**
(B) Brown water tower with gray roof and trim; brown switch tower with gray roof and trim; brown freight shed with gray roof and ends; four gray telephone poles; uncatalogued; 1960. **5 10 15**

0414 VILLAGE SET Thirty-seven-piece set, unpainted plastic; four telephone poles; four pine trees; twenty-four figures; a white theatre with gray roof and trim; white firehouse with red roof and trim; paints and brush included for decoration of figures; difficult to find complete set; catalogued in 1959 only. **15 20 25**

0415 CAPE COD SET Nineteen-piece set; house with white walls, brown roof, six green awnings, gray windows and doors; gray back porch with green roof; two white lounge chairs and table formed with porch; two telephone poles; two pine trees with brown trunks; six green foliage pieces for each tree; twelve sections of white picket fence and gate; difficult to find complete; catalogue incorrectly illustrated house with yellow or tan walls; these colors were not made for Lionel; catalogued in 1960-61. **5 10 15**

0416 STATION SET Twenty-piece set, unpainted plastic; white suburban station with brown roof and gray loading platform; gray windows and brown doors in station; Plasticville name boards on rooftop; two brown telephone poles; one black block signal; white crossing signal; twelve figures; paint set and brush included for figures; catalogued in 1960 only. **5 10 15**

0417 FARM SET Burgundy barn walls; gray barn and silo roofs; white house walls; brown roof and green awnings on house; gray porch with a table and two lounge chairs; green porch roof; two solid plastic pine trees; six chickens, a horse, three cows, two pigs, a sheep and lamb and one dog included; female figure and two pieces of green foliage also included; neither porch nor trees mentioned in catalogue; catalogued in 1960 only. **5 10 15**

0418 INDUSTRIAL SET Seven-piece set; white gas station with red roof and trim; two sets of gas pumps and two racks of oil cans; red automobile; tan factory with light gray roof and dark gray loading docks; gray factory doors and windows; matching water tower on factory roof; two brown telephone poles; catalogued in 1960. **3 5 10**

0419 RAIL JUNCTION SET Similar to 0413; gray coaling station with brown roofs and trim replaces water tank; six telephone poles; block signal; crossing signal; three figures; several barrels and crates; catalogued in 1960 only; difficult to find complete. **3 5 10**

0420 RAILROAD SET Similar to 0416; white station with brown roof and trim; four telephone poles; four pine trees; six separate foliage pieces for each tree; figures, paint set, block signal and crossing signal included, though not listed in catalogue; catalogued in 1961; difficult to find complete. **3 5 10**

0421 FARM SET Twenty-four-piece set; barn; farmhouse; white dog house, hen house and garage with red roofs; red corn crib with white roof; sixteen unpainted figures; catalogued in 1961-62; difficult to find complete.
(A) Burgundy barn with gray roof; white house with brown roof and trim; 1961. **5 10 15**
(B) White barn with red roof; matching house; 1962. **5 10 15**

0422 FREIGHT SET Twenty-six-piece set; gray water tower, coaling station, switch tower and freight station with brown roofs; set included new railroad work car built to resemble bunk car without wheels; work car has brown sides and a gray roof, rather than all-red color shown in catalogue; six telephone poles; four figures; several barrels and crates; one of the biggest catalogued sets; also most expensive, set sold for $5.00; catalogued in 1961-62. **5 10 15**

0425 FIGURE SETS Twenty-four figures and crossing gate; paint, thinner and brush included; catalogued in 1962-63. **3 5 10**

0426 RAILROAD STATION SET White suburban station with brown roof; platform added to station; four telephone poles; crossing gate; block signal; crossing signal; unpainted black plastic signal bridge; four figures; barrels, crates and bench; catalogued in 1962 only. **3 5 10**

TREES AND SCENERY

Catalogued from 1959 through 1962, these items are thought to be products of Life-Like Products in Baltimore, Maryland. However, this has not been confirmed. The items tend to be of little interest to collectors.

0430 TREES

0431 LANDSCAPE SET
0432 TREE ASSORTMENT
0433 SCENERY SET

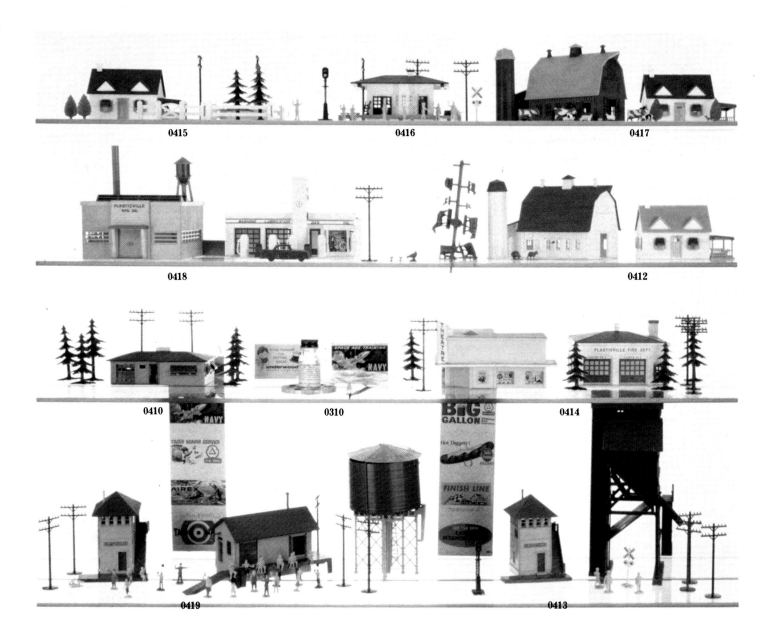

0415   0416   0417

0418   0412

0410   0310   0414

0419   0413

From 1959 through 1962, Bachmann supplied Lionel with many buildings from its H0 Plasticville line. Only a few of the many items were actually catalogued. On the top shelf are the 0415 Cape Cod Set (left) with nineteen pieces, the 0416 Station Set with twenty pieces (center) and the 0417 Farm Set with twenty-one pieces. On the left-hand side of the second shelf is the 0418 Industrial Area Set with seven pieces, including gas station with pumps, telephone poles and an automobile. Next to the industrial set is the 0412 Farm Set, which differs in color from the one shown above it. In the farm set, we show a jumbo Purdue chicken (alias Plasticville 0 Gauge) next to the tiny chickens that came with the set. The plastic sprue holding our farm animals in a most precarious way came only with the early sets.

The third shelf displays the 0410 Ranch House with accessories (left), two 0310 Billboards, and the thirty-seven piece 0414 Village Set, including the theatre, firehouse, people, trees, poles, palette, liquid paint thinner (Bachmann Styrene Painting Fluid) and brush. The bottom shelf displays the 0413 Railway Structure Set with seven pieces, including water and switch tower, freight shed and telephone poles. This set also came with the colors reversed (see text). The 0419 Rail Junction Set on the right came only in the colors shown. The set includes a coal tower, signal tower, six telephone poles, block signal, crossing signal and three figures. The set also includes barrels and crates, which are not shown here.

Chapter V
Collecting Lionel H0 Trains

LIONEL AND THE WIDE SCOPE OF H0 COLLECTING
By Vincent Rosa

Back in 1976, Howard Godel wrote a book called **Antique Toy Trains, The Hobby of Collecting Old Toy Trains.** In Chapter 12, he took a deep breath and projected his thoughts to the future. Under the heading of "sleepers" (items that have not yet become popular and tend to bring currently low prices), he states, "a series that is just beginning to be appreciated and is presently a sleeper are the small trains produced by Lionel and American Flyer in comparatively small quantities compared to their 0 and S Gauge production."[1] That prediction was written back in 1976! In 1986 we can safely say that the H0 series has become a Lionel collectible. Many of the early Lionel H0 items have appreciated as much as or beyond the value of similar 0 Gauge items. This statement may surprise some, but those of us who have been collecting Lionel H0 steadily for several years are not surprised at all.

H0 train buffs have become avid collectors. Some H0 enthusiasts complain that, "Lionel is not prototypically accurate." My rejoinder is, "Every stickler for H0 realism has at least one item he calls cute (which means unrealistic)." Just once, I would like to see a magazine such as **Model Railroader** show an absolutely prototypical train going through an exact scale Christmas-time countryside setting with a "blinking" Lionel atomic energy disposal car and a bobbing giraffe car at the tail of the consist. Imagine the letters the editor would receive in January if such an illustration appeared on the cover of the December issue!

Today, the H0 train buff has numerous possibilities from which to choose if he desires to collect H0 trains. He or she can specialize by collecting and concentrating on one specific manufacturer, such as Lionel (postwar 1957-1966 or MPC 1974-1977), Gilbert (American Flyer H0), Athearn, Hobbyline, Mantua, Marx (yes, Marx made H0 too), Penn Line, Revell, Rivarossi, Roundhouse, Varney, and many other domestic and foreign producers. Other choices open to the collector are catalogued and uncatalogued sets, custom-painted models, cabooses (cabeese ?), passenger trains or coal hoppers by the yard. Others may prefer to collect models carrying the name of a specific prototype railroad, such as Atlantic Coast Line, New York Central, Canadian Pacific or Virginian. Those who prefer the finest in H0 scale can purchase some of the brass models currently available or those that have been discontinued for several years. Brass is beautiful—and costly. Many collectors consider brass to be the champagne-and-caviar of H0 collecting. Regardless of the choice, the collector can go as far as time, money and imagination takes him.

Mass-market H0 trains, like Lionel produced after 1958, may have been subjected to collectors' sneers and scoffs when they were first released, but they are not being criticized today.

Lionel H0 models are quality products: well made, durable and ingeniously manufactured and designed. Also, many Lionel H0 pieces are difficult to collect because they are not around - for any price. Just try and locate a mint Matchbox bulldozer (Lionel 0807) or tractor on a flatcar (0808), a 0610 Lionel/ Rivarossi Consolidation Steamer from 1957 or the "Valise Pack" train set 5767 from 1961. These items are all scarce if not rare, and there are many others.

Lionel's postwar H0 items are part of H0's tinplate heritage as well as a part of the larger history of the Lionel Corporation itself. By 1962 more than fifty percent of all home train sets and layouts were in H0 scale, and almost all of these used compatible equipment produced by a variety of manufacturers.[2] It was inevitable that many of these "ready-to-run" items would become collectors' items. Lionel H0 was a sleeper whose awakening has come. Collecting Lionel H0 presents a great challenge, especially to those who want to pursue all phases and variations of production. Remember, challenges make collecting what it should be for all of us—fun!

The following guidelines will help you differentiate production by Rivarossi, Athearn and Lionel.

Three different Lionel derrick cars, made by Rivarossi (top), Athearn (center) and Lionel Corporation (bottom).

1. Godel, Howard. **Antique Toy Trains.** Exposition Press, Inc., Hicksville, NY. 1976. p. 207.

2. Revell 1962 H0 catalogue, advance issue.

Underside of a Rivarossi boxcar. Note receptacles for separate details, which do not appear on the cars sold by Lionel.

HOW TO RECOGNIZE LIONEL/RIVAROSSI H0

Rivarossi's production is somewhat easier to identify than that of Athearn or the Lionel Corporation. This production includes those items catalogued in 1957, and a few of the rolling stock pieces sold in 1958 or even later. Lionel/Rivarossi H0 can be differentiated from Lionel/Athearn and regular Lionel Corporation H0 as follows:

1. Use the 1957 catalogue selling sheet for reference.
2. Rivarossi pieces have the Rivarossi logo stamped underneath.
3. Most Rivarossi pieces also have the Lionel **L** (like Lionel/Athearn production pieces). This will differentiate Lionel pieces from regular Rivarossi production. However, in the rush to supply Lionel, Rivarossi packaged some items which did not have the logo.
4. Rivarossi boxcars have "model quality" detailing, such as separate roofwalks and fragile ladders.
5. See 1957 selling sheet for list of diesel road names.
6. The two Rivarossi steam engines are the 0600 Dockside Switcher and the 0610 LT Consolidation. Notes on this engine, according to the ones that exist in the Collections of Joseph Jerome and George Horan are:
- The single cab window has an arched top, typical of European style locomotives.
- Has turned brass bell; cab, boiler and tender shell are black painted plastic; locomotive frame is sheet metal and plastic.
- Full working valve gear.
- Tender number 280 in 5/16" lettering (catalogue shows no number on tender).
- Tender frame is die-cast, lettering on bottom reads:

Rivarossi

Como - Italia

1370

Made in Italy

- Motor is in tender with drive shaft to engine.
- Engine frame reads:

Rivarossi

Como - Italia

1515

Made in Italy

Castings on the tender were poor. This piece is extremely hard to find in good condition; it is a very scarce engine. It is advisable to purchase one in a Lionel/Rivarossi box, although there are not many to be found.

Note: The 0501 Fairbanks Morse Rivarossi diesel with the B unit is quite scarce. Be careful, as these units supposedly do not have a Lionel **L**. Buy a boxed piece if you can.

HOW TO RECOGNIZE
LIONEL/ATHEARN PRODUCTION

1. Use the 1958 consumer and advance catalogues as reference sources. If you have "mint" or boxed pieces, it will be very easy to cross-reference the catalogue numbers with those on the box. Only Athearn's road number appears on the piece.
2. Athearn pieces are not marked with an Athearn logo, but, on most rolling stock and engines, there appears an encircled **L**. Some Rivarossi pieces have this logo too. However, the Rivarossi pieces are distinguished by the appearance of that company's name on the underside of all rolling stock and locomotives.

Three different Lionel gondola cars. The Rivarossi model (top) is a 40 foot car with straight side sills. The Athearn model (center) is a 50 foot car with "fishbelly" sides. The Lionel model (bottom) is a 40 foot car with straight side sills; note that the ribs are spaced more closely than those on the Rivarossi model.

3. Lionel/Athearn H0 boxcar characteristics are easily recognized. Look for separate roofwalks (not molded in the roof), sprung trucks, black spray-painted weighted underframes, plastic "short pin" N.M.R.A. couplers rather than finger tab couplers (which have an extended piece of plastic to make manual uncoupling easier), thin plastic simulated steel doors and plastic door guides. Typical Athearn production boxcars are not numbered with the Lionel catalogue number. Examples: 0864-225 Central of Georgia; 0862-200 Monon boxcar.

4. Lionel/Athearn cabooses have many revealing characteristics. Underframes, trucks and couplers are screwed in place. Many do not have a "tab-slot" (visible tab which holds caboose body to frame). All have body-mounted couplers. The Lionel name and logo do not appear on the bottom of the split frame. The Athearn logo does not appear anywhere on the piece either. Usually there is a "Built by Lionel" or a Lionel **L** logo on each side of the piece.

Other characteristics to look for are separate roofwalks (not molded in roof), plastic brakewheels, metal railings and plastic smokestacks. Lionel numbers were stamped on some cabooses but not all. For example, one Rio Grande caboose is stamped 01439 on the side, but the number on the Lionel box is 0817-50. By the way, this is a mint piece; it clearly came with all railings, etc. but no smokestack. The Lionel Corporation often advertised in its instruction sheets that, for five cents or so, you could buy modeling parts to give your cabooses more detail. Many late Lionel Corporation H0 cabooses, such as the 0837 M.St.L., came without any detailing parts.

GENERAL NOTES AND COMMENTS
ON LIONEL/ATHEARN H0 PRODUCTION

Athearn produced H0 for Lionel from 1958 to 1960. The 1958 catalogues (advance and consumer) provide a useful guide. The airplane car, Lionel 0800, was shown in both the 1958 and 1959 catalogues; evidently, either production had continued or a quantity remained available. Some collectors have mentioned that Lionel/Athearn H0 has been known to come through without the Lionel **L** stamped on it. A collector should consider these pieces as genuine Lionel products only if he saw them in mint condition in an unopened Lionel box. Undoubtedly, some regular Athearn (unmarked with **L**) did slip by the factory workers and into Lionel boxes. But, one problem remains. If we allow all Athearn pieces (unboxed, etc.) to be considered Lionel, then who is to stop the unscrupulous individual from putting a 1950's Athearn caboose worth $3.00 into a Lionel box and getting $20.00 for it?

Another "gray" area for collectors is the Lionel/Athearn N.H. passenger cars series released in 1958. In this series, the numbers on the car sides are not the same as those used in the catalogues and on the cartons. (See our chronological list for all numbers.) For example, the 701 Pullman was actually numbered 3150. There are no Lionel logos reported on the pieces. Yet, the two F-7 New Haven diesels are numbered 0272 instead 0533, as found in the catalogue and on the box. Both have the Lionel **L** on them. Use extreme caution when purchasing Athearn pieces without a box. If the piece is "unboxed", only consider it a Lionel piece if it has the Lionel **L** (within a circle) on it.

Athearn made some pieces, or at least catalogued some pieces, in their own consumer catalogue that were also made for Lionel. Some recognizable pieces are the 0800 Airplane car,

0590 Virginian Rectifier and the 0866-25 Santa Fe stock car to name a few. Also, there is an 0864-50 State of Maine boxcar catalogued in 1957-1958. This "mint" boxed piece is clearly Athearn production. While Athearn and Rivarossi did duplicate some familiar paint schemes, such as that on the colorful State of Maine boxcars, in and after 1958, we are reasonably certain that all of the items depicted in Lionel's 1957 catalogue were produced by the latter.

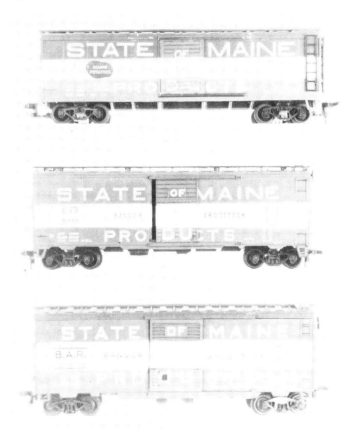

State of Maine boxcars by Rivarossi (top), Athearn (center) and Lionel (bottom).

All F-7s (1958) are clearly Athearn products with rubber belt drives. Of the Rectifier locomotives, only the 0590 is a product of the Athearn shop. Actually, the locomotive is a joint product, as Lionel had created the dies for the body shells. Subsequent releases of the Virginian locomotives feature a Lionel Corporation drive. The 0615 Boston & Maine Pacific would have been an Lionel/Athearn, but Athearn did not produce it in 1959, as scheduled. However, Athearn did release this model under its own label in 1962.

HOW TO RECOGNIZE LIONEL CORPORATION
PRODUCTION PIECES

1. Check consumer and advance catalogues from 1959-1966.
2. Lionel Corporation pieces all have the Lionel catalogue number on their sides. Some rolling stock has the number both on the sides and on the bottom, which is lettered "The Lionel Corporation/Made in the U.S. of America".
3. All operating rolling stock that mirrors the late 1950s through 1960s 0 Gauge line is clearly Lionel Corporation H0. Example: The 0805 Atomic Energy Disposal Car, 0333 Satellite

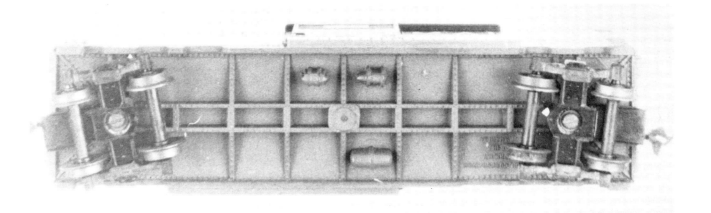

Underside of a boxcar manufactured by Lionel.

car, 0850 Missile Launcher, etc. This also applies to accessories such as the 0145 Gateman.

4. Rolling stock produced until 1962 has sprung trucks and the finger-tab version of the N.M.R.A. couplers. After 1962, these items were produced with solid frame trucks, which do not have real coil springs as found on the earlier metal sprung trucks.

5. There are two kinds of boxcars — early production and late production. Early boxcar examples are: 0864-900, 0864-700, 0864-325. A late boxcar is the green 0874 New York Central. The late boxcars have the Lionel number and steel bottoms similar to the 6464-100 O Gauge boxcars. There are no Lionel Corporation markings, just the Lionel number.

6. Use our inventory list for reference.

7. Early boxcars were made from Hobbyline dies.

8. Late boxcars resulted from Lionel's attempt to create a new boxcar with its own die work.

9. We believe that Lionel produced all of the Pacifics, as well as all Alcos, like the Alaska Railroad 0567, and all motorized units like the 0050 gang cars. Plastic components were made from the Hobbyline dies.

10. Bachmann "Plasticville" items were also packaged by Lionel.

11. Atlas also made track and bridges that were boxed by Lionel.

12. Track manufactured by Lionel bears the lettering "The Lionel Corp." on the underside.

CARTONS AND PACKAGING

SEPARATE ITEMS

In 1957, the first cartons used for separate H0 scale items differed little in appearance from Lionel's classic orange and white packaging. However, the H0 cartons featured a plastic window, which allowed the consumer to see the contents quite clearly. An engineer's face, pictured in black and white, appeared at the top of the window and on one side of the box; all other printing was black. A listing of items then available appeared on the back of the box. A dull white cardboard liner provided a nest for the item in each box. Catalogue numbers appeared in black numerals on each end. The Rivarossi models were packaged in this type of box, which then had "Made in Italy" on the back. Only slight changes were made when Lionel production shifted to Athearn in 1958. The words "H0 by Lionel" were added above the picture window on the front,

and an illustration of H0 accessories replaced the catalogue listing on back. The Lionel name and "U.S.A." first appeared on these cartons.

Some of the printing changed when Lionel assumed production of the line in 1960. The lettering and the illustrations were changed from black to bright blue, and the dull white liners were replaced by brighter white liners. Some of the cartons featured written descriptions of the products. A blue band with the phrase "The Leader in Model Railroading" was added to both sides. The rear of the carton now featured a picture of an F-unit diesel and caboose. "Lionel" and "Hillside, NJ" also appear on the carton. The catalogue numbers on the box ends were changed to black. However, many of the cartons made for one product were used for another. In most cases, the original stamping was covered with a white paper sticker, which was stamped with the new number. Other times, a long blue line covered the old number, so that a new number could be stamped above or below it. Cartons for accessories were generally similar to those used for rolling stock items.

SET BOXES

Lionel employed a wider range of colors, shapes and sizes in creating the boxes for its train sets. In 1957, the company packaged sets in a dull yellow box with black printing. Then, in 1958, it switched to a gaudy orange, yellow and green box, which also had black printing. The sets contained individual cartons for each component; these cartons contained yellow

End view of a Rivarossi boxcar (left), Athearn boxcar (center) and Lionel boxcar made from Hobbyline dies (right).

liners, rather than the white liners used for individual items. The boxes had a fold back top (for countertop display), with the words "LIONEL H0" and the slogan "The Leader in Model Railroading." Set numbers appeared on the outer box. In 1959, Lionel again changed the boxes, this time to a bright yellow with a smaller "LIONEL H0" printed in red letters on the box top. The boxtop illustration depicts a Santa Fe Alco crossing a trestle and a steam locomotive and snow blower operating on a lower track. The 1959 box retained the foldback design and black printing.

In 1960, the company changed the color of the box to orange and white and added a large white "H0" with a black "LIONEL" stamped across it. An illustration of a Pacific steam locomotive, printed in gray, appeared on the top; all other printing remained black. Some of these cartons had orange or gray liners with holes punched to accept the items of the sets. Others continued to house separate boxes for the individual components. The box design changed in 1964, when Lionel discontinued the two-part design. The company continued to use the "Lionel H0" logo and the illustration of the Pacific locomotive, however only the box top remained orange. The remainder of the box was flat off-white. A white liner with punched holes held the components of each set.

The early sets with Athearn cars and Lionel locomotives were packaged in bright yellow boxes approximately one foot square and six inches high. Very few sets were packaged in the flat freight set-type box, which had "LIONEL H0" in red letters and the set description and catalogue number in black. The front and back of this carton were imprinted with the illustration from the cover of the 1957 catalogue. Later passenger sets were packaged in bright orange cartons approximately the same size. The printing on these boxes was all black, and only the Lion's head trademark and the slogan "An Investment in Happiness" appeared on the box top. Individual component boxes were included in each of the foregoing box types.

Several variations of the basic designs were used throughout Lionel's production of H0. For example, set 14310 had an orange and gray box with black lettering. This box, circa 1965-1966, depicts an 0 Gauge steam locomotive with a square tender pulling a 6464-475 boxcar and a 6631 log car. A paper tag with a description and illustration of the set contents is located on the side of the box. Santa Fe freight set 14310-502, with a 0595 diesel, was sold in a square cardboard box with "LIONEL TRAINS" stamped on it in black; the box is also lettered "Guaranteed and Manufactured by the Lionel Corp., N.Y., N.Y." in black letters. Co-author Vincent Rosa, who owns both of these example sets, notes that the latter set may have been one of the last to leave the Lionel plant at Hillside, New Jersey.

REPRODUCTION BOXES

It has come to the attention of both authors that a dealer has had made a box which very closely reproduces the original Lionel cartons. The reproduction cartons have lighter construction (thinner cardboard and clear plastic) than the originals, but they are in no way marked to indicate that they are reproductions.

These boxes, which are used for single items, are rubber stamped such that they may be differentiated from the original cartons. The originals have thin lettering with crisp edges, whereas the reproductions have fat lettering with weak edges. Most of the original boxes are heat stamped. Lionel did rubber stamp a few boxes, but items like the 0057 Air Force switcher did not come in rubber-stamped boxes. The boxes first appeared in mid-1985, and they add to the price being asked for the items. The reproductions currently available have cardboard liners inside and the late style picture, showing the diesel, caboose and the Pacific set going through the girder bridge, on the back. Unfortunately, **collectors must now inspect the cartons before making a purchase**.

Chapter VI
Catalogued Sets

The following listings indicate for each set the catalogue number, the road name, the locomotive(s), the number of cars and the year in which the set was sold or catalogued.

PASSENGER SETS

Presented in ascending numerical order.

5714   **NEW HAVEN** 0533 F7-A powered, 0553 A dummy; three cars; 1958.

5732   **TEXAS SPECIAL**   0566 Alco A powered, 0576 B dummy and 0586 A dummy; four cars; 1959.

5742   **PENNSYLVANIA**   0581 Rectifier; three cars; 1960.

5756   **SOUTHERN PACIFIC** 0635 Pacific; three cars; 1961.

5759   **SANTA FE** 0565 Alco A powered, 0595 A dummy; four cars; 1961.

5770   **TEXAS SPECIAL**   Two 0566 Alco A powered, 0576 B dummy; four cars; 1960.

14054   **TEXAS SPECIAL**   0566 Alco A powered; four cars; 1962.
(A) As catalogued with a baggage car, two Dome cars and an observation car.
(B) Three Dome cars and an observation; cardboard insert die-cut for three Dome cars; no short opening for baggage car; D. MacNary Collection; J. Fulton comment.

14108   **SANTA FE** 0535 Alco A powered, 0575 B dummy; four cars; 1962.

14163   **PENNSYLVANIA**   0571 Alco A powered; three cars; 1963.

14290   **SANTA FE** 0555 Alco A powered; three cars; 1964.

14320   **SANTA FE**
(A) 0555 Alco A powered, 0575 B dummy; three cars; 1965.
(B) 0556 Alco A powered; three cars; 1966.

FREIGHT SETS

Note: "FM" stands for Fairbanks Morse diesel.

1957

5700   (UNLETTERED) 0000 switcher; three cars.

5701   **ILLINOIS CENTRAL** 0505 FM A powered; five cars.

5702   **WABASH** 0502 FM A powered, 0522 B dummy; five cars.

5703   **WESTERN PACIFIC** 0503 FM A powered, 0523 B dummy and 0513 A dummy; five cars.

5704   (UNLETTERED) 0610 Consolidation; six cars.

1958

5705   **U.S. NAVY** 0570 Husky; four cars.

5707   **WABASH** 0580 GP-9; four cars.

5709   **MILWAUKEE ROAD** 0531 F-7A; five cars.

5711   **VIRGINIAN** 0590 Rectifier; six cars.

5713   **BALTIMORE & OHIO** 0532 F-7A powered, 0542 B dummy; five cars.

5715   **RIO GRANDE** 0530 F-7A powered; five cars.

5717   **BOSTON & MAINE** 0615 Pacific, which was never made; six cars; not manufactured; see 1959 sets.

1959

5717   **SOUTHERN PACIFIC** 0625 Pacific; six cars.

5719   **A.E.C.** 0056 Husky; three cars.

5721   **TEXAS SPECIAL** 0566 Alco A unit; four cars.

5723   (UNLETTERED) 0605 Steam switcher; four cars.

5725   **NEW HAVEN** 0591 Rectifier; five cars.

5727   **NEW YORK CENTRAL** 0596 GP-9; five cars.

5729   **ALASKAN** 0567 Alco A powered, 0577 B dummy; five cars.

5731   **SOUTHERN PACIFIC** 0625 Pacific; five cars.

5733   **SANTA FE** 0565 Alco A powered, 0575 B dummy and 0595 A dummy; seven cars.

1960

5735   **ROCK ISLAND** 0058 Husky; three cars.

5737   (UNLETTERED) 0602 Steam switcher; four cars.

5739   **C&O** 0564 Alco A; four cars.

5741   **PENNSYLVANIA** 0602 Steam switcher; four cars.

5743   **NORTHERN PACIFIC** 0597 GP-9; five cars.

5745   **SOUTHERN PACIFIC** 0625 Pacific; five cars.

5747   **SANTA FE** 0565 Alco A powered, 0575 B dummy; five cars.

5749   **PENNSYLVANIA** 0602 Steam switcher; six cars.

5771   **SOUTHERN PACIFIC** 0625 Pacific; six cars.

1961

5750   **M.St.L.** 0055 Husky; three cars.

5751   **ERIE** 0545 G.E. Switcher; three cars.

This Athearn Boston & Maine Pacific is similar to the one that would have appeared in set 5717 had Athearn produced this model in 1958.

0643 Steam switcher from set 14133.

5752 (UNLETTERED) 0642 Steam switcher; four cars.

5753 C&O 0564 Alco A; four cars.

5754 SOUTHERN PACIFIC 0625 Pacific; five cars.

5755 NEW YORK CENTRAL 0598 GP-7; five cars.

5757 SOUTHERN PACIFIC 0635 Pacific; five cars.

5758 SANTA FE 0565 Alco A powered, 0575 B dummy; six cars.

5762 SOUTHERN PACIFIC 0635 Pacific; seven cars.

5767 (UNLETTERED) 0642 Steam switcher; three cars.

1962

14003 M.St.L. 0055 Husky; three cars.

14013 ERIE 0545 GE Switcher; three cars.

14023 (UNLETTERED) 0642 Steam switcher; four cars.

14033 UNION PACIFIC 0568 Alco A; four cars.

14043 SOUTHERN PACIFIC 0636 Pacific; four cars.

14064 NORTHERN PACIFIC 0597 GP-9; five cars.

14074 SOUTHERN PACIFIC 0645 Pacific; four cars.

14084 SANTA FE 0535 Alco A powered; 0535W A dummy with horn; 0370 Sheriff and Outlaw Car; 0865-335 Gondola with scrap metal; 0845 Gold Bullion Car; 0821-110 Pipe Car; 0841-185 Caboose; J. Otterbein and J. Kimenhour Collections.

14087 SANTA FE 0535 Alco A powered, 0536W B dummy; five cars.

14098 SOUTHERN PACIFIC 0645 Pacific; five cars.

1963

14133 (UNLETTERED) 0643 Steam switcher; three cars.

14143 SANTA FE 0594 GP-9 (incorrectly catalogued as GP-7); five cars.

14153 SOUTHERN PACIFIC 0626 Pacific; six cars.

14173 SANTA FE 0555 Alco A powered, 0595 A dummy; four cars.

14183 SOUTHERN PACIFIC 0635 Pacific; eight cars.

14193 NORTHERN PACIFIC 0593 GP-9 powered, 0593T dummy; seven cars.

14203 SANTA FE 0536 Alco A powered, 0535 B dummy and 0595 A dummy; seven cars.

14233 SOUTHERN PACIFIC 0646 Pacific; eight cars.

1964-1966

14240 M.St.L. 0055 Husky; three cars; 1964-66.

14260 SANTA FE
(A) 0594 GP-9; four cars; 1964-65.
(B) 0592 GP-9; four cars; 1966.

14270 SOUTHERN PACIFIC 0626 Pacific; four cars; 1964.

14280 SOUTHERN PACIFIC 0636 Pacific; six cars; 1964-66.

14300 SOUTHERN PACIFIC
(A) 0646 Pacific; seven cars; 1964-65.
(B) 0647 Pacific; six cars; 1966.

14310 SANTA FE 0550 Alco A powered, 0535 B dummy and 0595 A dummy; seven cars; 1964-66.

UNCATALOGUED SETS

Lionel catalogued many train sets between 1957 and 1966, but there are at least a few sets that were not catalogued. The authors invite collectors to report full details, including set number and set name (if any), locomotives and rolling stock found in set and a description of the packaging and enclosed literature. The following is an example of an uncatalogued set that has been reported.

5760 SENTINEL Union Pacific Husky locomotive; Exploding Boxcar; U.S. Missile Launching Car; A.E.C. Car; Union Pacific caboose; reported by J. Fulton, J. Otterbein and J. Kimenhour; c. 1960.

Chapter VII
Trucks, Mechanisms and Frames

DIESEL TRUCKS

The GP diesels and Rectifier electric manufactured for Lionel by Athearn in 1958-59 employed Athearn's Hi-F drive, which utilized neoprene bands to transmit power from the drive shaft to the drums on the axles, such as those found on this Athearn truck.

This truck appears in both powered and dummy versions of the Alco diesel manufactured by Lionel, 1960-63. Powered models featured a Helic drive and neoprene drive bands. Dummy models were assembled without drive bands or gears.

Truck for Lionel dummy GP and Alco locomotives, 1963.

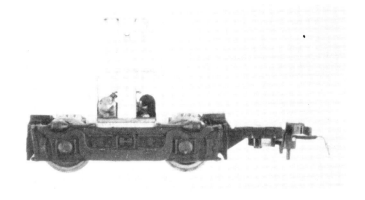

Lionel used a four-axle, truck-mounted drive with a gear box in 1964-65. This unit has rubber traction tires on the forward axle.

The trucks on Rivarossi FM diesel locomotives were painted to match the colors on the bodies of the locomotives. This truck came from an FM dummy.

The direct gear drive featured on the 0592 Santa Fe GP-9. This unit has two rubber tires on the rear wheels.

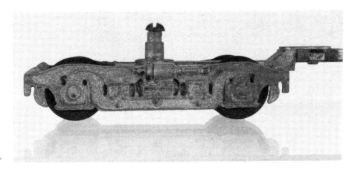

Athearn passenger car truck.

Here is a freight car truck made by Lionel in 1959. This truck has a metal coupler cover with a hole at the top. This is part number 0866-50 in the Lionel service manual.

The truck from an observation car made by Lionel is listed in the service manual as part number 0715-50.

The freight car truck from 1960-1963 differs slightly from the 1959 truck. It has a solid coupler cover, without the hole found on the earlier version.

The sprung truck used on cabooses manufactured by Lionel has plastic side frames.

This is the metal collector-type truck used on operating cars and cabooses for which electrical collection from the track is needed to light or operate the cars.

Sprung truck from a Lionel/Athearn freight car.

After 1963, Lionel used this metal truck with a manual uncoupler pivot pin.

A view of the mechanism from the 0602 steam locomotive manufactured by Lionel.

Mechanism from the diminutive 0605 steam locomotive manufactured by Lionel.

The mechanisms of Lionel's 2-4-2 steam switchers appear similar at first glance, but there are subtle differences. The 0642 (shown above) has both a drive rod and a connecting rod, while the 0643 (shown below) has only a drive rod. The 0643 has a bulge in the frame, just above the space between the two drivers, that does not appear on the 0642.

Mechanism of the 0643 steam switcher manufactured by Lionel.

The mechanisms of the 0625 steam locomotive changed slightly between 1959 and 1960. The earlier version (shown above) is obviated by the smaller opening in the weight, above the center driver. The latter version (shown below) has a larger opening, as well as a slower gear ratio, which may be obviated by inspecting the gears.

Mechanism of the 0625 steam locomotive manufactured in 1960.

This mechanism is typical of the steam locomotives with smoke units, which include 0635, 0636, 0637, 0645, 0646 and 0647. Motors, frames and bearings varied during the course of Lionel's production.

Steam locomotive motors. The late motor, used on all four- and six-driver switchers, appears at left. (Note that the 0605 may be found with either late or early motors.) The early motor, which has a single screw above the armature shaft, appears on the unit in the middle of the photograph. At right is the late motor, as mounted in a Pacific locomotive chassis, with two screws above the armature shaft.

Shown on the top shelf is the mechanism of the band-driven Alco locomotive, manufactured 1959-61. The bands, which are missing from this sample fit on the pulleys at either end of the drive shaft. A heftier version of the band-driven Alco mechanism appears on the second shelf. This model has additional weight, on the frame at each end of the motor cavity, and heavier drive shafts. The mechanism of a gear-driven Alco locomotive with rear-truck drive, produced in 1964, appears on the bottom shelf.

A typical 1965 Alco dummy unit frame.

Shown here are motors from various locomotives. At top left is the motor for the Athearn units with Hi-F (rubber band) drive. The motor at top center is part number 0565-200 (listed as 0565-000 after 1960), which is used in the following locomotives: 0581, 0591, 0596, 0597 and 0598; these are described in Chapter 4. The motor at top right is representative of the late motor used on the 0625 and 0635 steam locomotives in 1960; it is part number 0635-202. At bottom left is part number 0642-200, which is the motor used in 2-4-2 steam switchers from 1961 to 1963. At bottom center is part number 0565, which powers some 1959 and all 1960 0625 locomotives. Finally, at bottom right, is the motor used in all husky locomotives produced by Lionel; it is part number 0056-28.

This frame appears on the 5095 Santa Fe Alco dummy, 1964-65. The factory ground the weight and truck-mounting portions from the frame to reduce the weight of the unit.

Chapter VIII
Catalogues and Paper Items

By I.D. Smith
With the assistance of Robert J. Osterhoff

Gd VG Exc Mt

1957

ADVANCE CATALOGUE: 11" x 8-1/4", 54 pages, red and black covers, black and white coated stock.   5   10   15   20

AND NOW H0—BY LIONEL: 10-3/4" x 7-5/8", "For the Discriminating Hobbyist...", supplement to Advance Catalogue, four-page color folder, may have been distributed separately and/or in consumer catalogue in addition to Advance Catalogue.   .25   .50   1   2

CATALOGUE: 11-1/4" x 7-1/2", 52 pages, full color, coated stock, cover has "New Super '0' Track".   1   2   3   7

ACCESSORY CATALOGUE: With Service Station Directory for 1957-58, 10" x 7-1/2", 32 pages, red and black covers, black and white pulp paper.   .25   .50   1   2

HOW TO OPERATE LIONEL TRAINS AND ACCESSORIES: 8-1/2" x 5-1/2", 64 black and white pages plus red and black wraparound cover, pulp paper.   .25   .50   1   2

BANNER: H0 BY LIONEL THE LEADER IN MODEL RAILROADING 21-3/16" x 6-1/2", 32 pages, red and black covers, black and white pulp paper.   .50   1   2   3

1958

ADVANCE CATALOGUE: 10-7/8" x 8-1/4", 64 pages, red and black cover, NH and M&StL trains passing missile launching site, black and white, H0 scale section (pages 50-55) has burgundy marker with gold-stamped "H0".

5   10   15   20

CATALOGUE: 11-1/4" x 7-5/8", 56 pages, cover like Advance Catalogue but in full color on coated stock.   2   4   6   8

ACCESSORY CATALOGUE: With Service Station Directory, 11-1/8" x 8", 32 pages, red and black cover, black and white, pulp paper. Title "Lionel 1958 Accessory Catalogue" contains individual items only. Cover picture is similar to regular catalogue, inside front cover copyrighted 1958. Weber Collection.   .50   1   2   3

ADVANCE H0 CATALOGUE: 10-7/8" x 8-1/8", eight pages, black and white, cover has red background and illustration of H0 display, rear cover shows dealer displays "For Your H0 Department".   .50   1   2   3

H0 CATALOGUE:
(A) 8-1/8" x 10-7/8", six-page fold-out, full color, coated stock.
.50   1   2   3
(B) 8-1/4" x 11-1/4", eight pages, full color, coated stock.
.50   1   2   3
(C) 8" x 11", six-page fold-out, full color, coated stock, copyright 1958 by The Lionel Corporation. Published in **Railroad Model Craftsman** magazine, October 1958, as unnumbered pages 35 through 40, and in Fall 1958 issue of **Model Trains** magazine.   1   2   3   4

PRIVATE CATALOGUE: "Lionel 1958", large eight-page illustrated edition, as issued by Ray's Bike & Key Shop, Geneva, New York. Features 2018 locomotive with tender on cover, in red and black on newsprint paper. Osterhoff Collection.   NRS

1959

ADVANCE CATALOGUE: 8-1/2" x 10-7/8", 44 pages, full color, black and white, fold-out pages, coated stock, cover lettered "Lionel 1959", illustration shows 1872 General and 44 missile launcher.   3   7   12   18

CATALOGUE: 11" x 8-1/2", 56 pages, full color, coated stock, cover illustration shows 736, 1872 General and 44 U.S. Army; H0 featured on pages 48-55.
(A) U.S. Edition, with prices.   3   5   9   12
(B) Canadian Edition, without prices; two-page insert, "Lionel Trains Canadian Price List 1959"; Osterhoff collection.   NRS

ACCESSORY CATALOGUE: 11" high x 8" wide, red and black front cover with 1872 and 44 locomotives, black ink only on pulp interior pages, 36 pages. Schreiner Collection.   .75   1.50   2   3

H0 CATALOGUE: 8-1/8" x 11", eight pages, full color, coated stock, copyright 1958 by The Lionel Corporation, published in **Railroad Model Craftsman** magazine, October 1959, as unnumbered pages 35 through 42, and in Fall 1959 issue of **Model Trains** magazine.   1   2   3   4

PRIVATE CATALOGUE: "Lionel 1959 Trains and Accessories", published by Distributors' Promotions, Inc., Philadelphia. Red and black on white cover, 20 pages. Osterhoff Collection.   NRS

WINDOW POSTER: 22" x 9", "H0 by Lionel", full color, illustrating H0 motor and truck. Included in 1959 dealer promotional kit. Osterhoff Collection.   2   4   6   8

WINDOW POSTER: 22" x 9", "H0 by Lionel", full color illustrating H0 engines, set. Included in 1959 dealer promotional kit. Osterhoff Collection.
2   4   6   8

1960

ADVANCE CATALOGUE: 8-1/2" x 11", 60 pages, color cover, black and white, red and white back cover with promotional slogan, coated stock, cover illustration shows father and son viewing twin railroad layout.
(A) "Lionel 1960" cover, dark brown heading.   3   5   7   12
(B) "Lionel 1960" cover, red-orange heading. Osterhoff Collection.   NRS

CATALOGUE: 11" x 8-3/8", 56 pages, full color, coated stock, cover illustration shows family viewing close-up section of twin railroad layout; H0 section on pages 44-54.   3   5   9   12

ACCESSORY CATALOGUE: With Service Station listing, 8-5/8" x 11", 40 pages, color cover, black and white pulp paper.   1   2   3   4

HOW TO OPERATE LIONEL TRAINS AND ACCESSORIES:
(A) 8-1/2" x 5-3/8", 64 black and white pages on coated stock, heavy paper wraparound cover in black and white with red background, Form 926-60.
1   2   3   4
(B) Cover shows black and white photo of N & W Y6b, left and rear side with orange-red right half with black and white lettering, 62 pages, copyrighted 1960 inside rear cover. Smith and Weber Collections.
1   2   3   4

LIONEL TRACK LAYOUTS FOR "027", SUPER "0" AND H0 GAUGES, START BUILDING YOURS TODAY! 8-3/8" x 11", four pages, not numbered.
(A) Price 10 cents on front, page 2 has "1-115" on lower right, heavy white paper. "Address inquiries to: Lionel Service, Dept 74-E, Hoffman Place, Hillside, NJ 07205" on back page. Smith Collection.   .25   .50   .75   1
(B) Similiar to (A), but no price, no number, coated paper stock. On bottom last three pages concerning inquiries, "simply write to: Engineer Bill c/o The Lionel Corp., 15 East 26th St., New York, 10 NY." Smith Collection.
.25   .50   .75   1

H0 CATALOGUE: 8-1/2" x 10-7/8", 12 pages, full color, coated stock, cover reads, "Operating Cars - 1960's Most Exciting H0 News".
1   2   3   4

HOW TO OPERATE LIONEL H0 TRAINS: 8-1/2" x 5-1/2", 24 pages plus red and black covers. .50 1 2 3

WINDOW STREAMER: "See...Get...Brand New Operating Cars - Lionel H0", 22" x 8-1/2", black and red on white glossy paper. Included in 1960 dealer promotional kit. Osterhoff Collection. 2 4 6 8

STORE POSTER: "Vital Small Parts" and "Control and Operating Accessories for H0 by Lionel", 20" x 14", black on white paper. Included in 1960 dealer promotional kit. Osterhoff Collection. 1 2 3 4

1961

ADVANCE CATALOGUE: 8-1/2" x 11", 76 pages, John Bruce Medaris on color cover, black and white coated stock.
(A) Pages numbered, page 3 begins "Cleared For Immediate Release". 3 5 7 10
(B) Pages not numbered, page 3 begins with letter dated 1 Aug '60 from Medaris; Pre-1961 Toy Show Edition. 5 8 12 16

CATALOGUE: H0 section on pages 60-70.
(A) 8-1/2" x 11", 56 pages, layout and science sets on cover, red and black covers, inside black and white pulp paper, "Honorary Stockholder" on rear cover. .50 1 2 3
(B) 8-1/2" x 11", 72 pages, cover same as (A), but catalogue differs, full color coated stock, H0 raceways on rear cover. 1 2 4 6
(C) 8-1/2" x 11", 72 pages, H0 raceways on rear cover, but Canadian Edition. No prices published in catalogues, but does include a separate four-page flyer "Canadian Price List 1961". Osterhoff Collection. — — — 15

DEALER WINDOW POSTER: 21-1/2" x 9", "H0 By Lionel - The Leader in Model Railroading". Black and red on yellow rag paper. Included in 1961 dealer promotion kit. Osterhoff Collection. 2 4 6 8

LIONEL TRACK LAYOUTS FOR "027", SUPER "0" AND H0 GAUGES, START BUILDING YOURS TODAY!: 8-3/8" x 11", four pages not numbered. Included in 1961 dealer promotion kit. Osterhoff Collection. 1 2 3 4

1962

CATALOGUE: 8-1/2" x 11", 100 pages, cover lettered "Lionel 1962". 1 2 4 6

ADVANCE CATALOGUE: "Lionel Trains and Accessories - The Leader in Model RR 1962", 64 pages, four color cover, black and white inside, includes displays and H0. 8-1/2" x 11" vertical.
(A) First Edition Pre-Toy Show; bright blue cover, back page "Three Powerful New Lionel Lines". Osterhoff Collection. NRS
(B) Second Edition; dull blue cover, back page "Four Powerful New Lionel Lines". Osterhoff Collection. NRS

ACCESSORY CATALOGUE: 8-3/8" x 10-7/8".
(A) 62 pages, full color cover, first two and last two pages are coated stock, rest is black and white pulp. Ocilka Collection. NRS
(B) 40 pages, red and black cover, black and white, pulp paper. 1 2 3 4

CONTROL AND OPERATING ACCESSORIES FOR H0 BY LIONEL: Sales sheet, printed one side only, 20" x 14", black on white paper, lists No. 928 Maintenance Kit at $2.50. Included in 1962 dealer promotion kit. Osterhoff Collection. 1 2 3 4

LIONEL TRACK LAYOUTS FOR "'027", SUPER "0" AND H0 GAUGES, START BUILDING YOURS TODAY!: 8-3/8" x 11", four pages not numbered. Included in 1962 dealer promotion kit. Osterhoff Collection. 1 2 3 4

ADVERTISING PROOF SHEETS: 11" x 17", black on white high-gloss paper, complete set of ad mats for all products. Printed one side only.
(A) "0" and "027" trains, eight pages. Osterhoff Collection. — — — 35
(B) "H0" trains, six pages. Osterhoff Collection. NRS
(C) Lionel-Tri-Ang Scalextric, two pages. Osterhoff Collection. — — — 10
(D) Lionel-Spear Line, two pages. Osterhoff Collection. — — — 10
(E) Lionel's New Line of Science Sets, seven pages. Osterhoff Collection. — — — 22

1963

CATALOGUE: 8-3/8" x 10-7/8", 56 pages, color cover, red and black interior coated stock . 1 2 4 6

ADVANCE CATALOGUE: "Lionel 1963", 8-1/2" x 11", 80 pages, yellow, black and white cover, interior black and white, includes trains, Lionel-Porter and racing sets, etc. Smith and Zydlo Collections. NRS

ACCESSORY CATALOGUE: With Service Station listing, 8-3/8" x 10-7/8", 40 pages, blue and black cover, interior black and white pulp paper. .50 1 2 3

1964

CATALOGUE: 8-3/8" x 10-7/8", 24 pages, black and blue.
(A) Pulp paper, page 13 lists 6402 flatcar at $2.50. 1 2 4 5
(B) Same as (A), but 6402 is incorrectly listed at $3.95. 1 2 4 5
(C) Same as (A), but coated stock. 1 2 5 7
(D) Same as (B), but coated stock. 1 2 5 7

1965

CATALOGUE: 8-1/2" x 10-7/8", 40 pages, multi-color printing and backgrounds.
(A) Pulp paper. 1 2 4 5
(B) Coated stock. 1 2 5 7
(C) Same as (A), 6119 and 6401 (errata). 1 2 4 5
(D) Same as (B), 6119 and 6401 (errata). 1 2 5 7

HOW TO OPERATE LIONEL TRAINS: 8-1/2" x 11", 32 pages, black and white plus yellow wraparound cover, uncoated paper. .50 1 2 3

1966

ADVANCE CATALOGUE: 19-7/8" x 8-1/2", 40 pages, full color coated stock front and back cover, but unlike the consumer edition, front color is deep blue rather than purple. Page 2 printed "Advance Catalog" and all inside pages are black and white. Osterhoff Collection. NRS

CATALOGUE 10-7/8" x 8-3/8", 40 pages, full color coated stock, cover illustration shows father and son watching trains rush past.
(A) Set illustrations on pages 8 and 10. .50 1 2 3
(B) No illustrations as in (A). .50 1 2 3

Glossary

PART NO.	PART NAME	ILLUSTRATION	PRICE	WHERE USED
0766-5	Coupler		.15	1959 Freight Trucks 1959 Locomotives 1959-60 "Husky" Locos
0766-51	Coupler		.15	1960 Freight Trucks 1961 Passenger & Freight
0565-61	Coupler		.15	1960 Locomotives 1961 Locomotives
0705-6	Coupler		.15	1959-60 Passenger Cars

Advance catalogue A catalogue sent to dealers prior to release of consumer catalogue for a given year; Lionel used this tool to obtain advance reservations for new items; items which did not receive sufficient interest would be omitted from the consumer catalogue.

Axle drum A large piece placed over axles on the Athearn Hi-F diesels to effect a better reduction in speed.

Body-mounted (couplers) Couplers housed in a pocket attached to or molded on car floor; opposite of talgo type.

Cast-on (detail) A detail apparent on a part, such as body shell; opposite of separate detail parts, which are molded or cast individually and added to the main body.

Chemically blackened (metal part) A part which has been colored black by use a of a chemical process rather than painting.

Decorative horn A scale model of the horn found on prototype locomotives; the decorative horn, as distinct from an electrical horn placed inside the unit to produce actual sounds, serves only to enhance the realism of the model.

Four-number board door A boxcar door with four flat panels on which numbers or lettering are applied.

Gang car A small railway vehicle generally used for transportation of maintenance and inspection personnel.

Helic drive New in 1963, when Lionel replaced rubber drive belt in its 1959 mechanism with "Helic Spring" drive belt; belt transmits power from motor shaft to nylon worm gear in each truck; secondary shafts drive gears on axles at a 10:1 ratio.

Hi-F drive The Athearn locomotive mechanism of the late 1950s; uses rubber belts to transmit power from the drive shaft to the axles.

Horn hook coupler The standard coupler used by most manufacturers of H0 scale trains; designated "X2f" by the National Model Railroad Association; also called "N.M.R.A." couplers.

Mallory magnetic coupler Variation of the X-2f coupler; long lateral pin extending from shank added to enhance uncoupling characteristics; entered into production in 1962.

Neoprene belts Drive bands employed in locomotives using Athearn's Hi-F drive and Lionel's power trucks from 1959 to 1963.

Pantograph The electrical collector found atop Rectifier locomotives.

Rigid frame truck A freight or passenger car truck lacking of an equalization mechanism, such as a set of springs; generally, a one-piece plastic truck frame with separate wheel sets.

Silk-screened lettering Lettering applied by a painting process, in which the a silk screen is employed; the screen serves as a negative to the lettering, thus paint forced through the screen forms the lettering on the model.

Smoke unit An accessory devise used to generate smoke in steam locomotive models.

Sprung truck A freight or passenger car truck with springs as found on prototype cars; provides equalization for all axles.

Stamped lettering Lettering which is applied directly to item with an inked positive pad, usually rubber.

Talgo truck A freight or passenger car truck with coupler pocket attached.